IRELAND

IRELAND

Christianity discredited or pilgrim's progress?

Robin Boyd

BOOK SERIES

WCC Publications, Geneva

Cover design: Rob Lucas

Cover photo: Len Sirman Press

ISBN 2-8254-0922-7

© 1988 WCC Publications, World Council of Churches,
150, route de Ferney, 1211 Geneva 20, Switzerland

No. 37 in the Risk book series

Printed in Switzerland

Table of contents

Preface

I was born in Belfast, and grew up there, as a member of the Presbyterian Church in Ireland, into whose ministry I was ordained in 1951. After many years of service in North India and Australia I had the great privilege, in 1980, of returning to Ireland for seven years, as director of the Irish School of Ecumenics. Those years reinforced my conviction that Irish men and women, Protestant and Roman Catholic, North and South, *can* live together in Christian koinonia. I was surrounded by groups in which I could see such fellowship in action, often in the most difficult circumstances.

Yet there was division inside the churches, as well as between them, and my own was no exception. In the story which follows I have concentrated more on that church than the others, and if my criticism may sometimes seem harsh, it is because I love the church of my birth, and believe that it has a great role to play in the better Ireland of the future. One of the fascinating features of my recent years in Ireland was the opportunity to witness at close quarters the not dissimilar theological and ecumenical struggle going on in the Roman Catholic Church. What a liberation it is when, instead of confronting each other in barren controversy, we can witness to each other in love from within the koinonia, and enjoy a communion which is not yet complete but none the less real.

I have written about only a few of the many people and groups who are working for — and living — the new koinonia in Ireland. In particular I have limited myself to the four largest churches, and am conscious that I have neglected others, especially the distinctive witness of the Quakers, who have promoted many initiatives for peace. For that I apologise.

Irish Roman Catholics like to be called simply Catholics: Irish Protestants prefer to say Roman Catholic. Believing that we should listen to people's self-definition, I have used both terms. For the same reason I have referred to the famous city on the Foyle as both Derry and Londonderry.

What I say in the following pages represents my personal views, and should not be attributed to the Irish School of Ecumenics or any of the other communities and groups with which I have been associated. As I now stand back from the

Irish scene and reflect on it from the very different setting of the Uniting Church in Australia, I believe that Ireland has a message for the worldwide church: a warning, indeed; but also a message of hope.

Melbourne   Robin Boyd
March 1988

1. Images of a Community Divided

A car careers out of control down a Belfast street. Its driver, a republican paramilitary, has been hit by gunfire from a British army patrol. A woman with three children is walking along the pavement and the car slams into them. The woman is badly injured, but survives: the three children are killed. It is August 1976, and the "Troubles" in Northern Ireland have been going on for eight years. People have had enough, and when Mairead Corrigan, sister of the bereaved mother, joins forces with her friend Betty Williams to rouse Belfast women — Catholic and Protestant — against the violence, she finds a heart-warming response, and the group known as the Peace People emerges.

... Yet in 1988, after twenty years of the Troubles, the violence still continues...

* * *

It is 1981, and in the so-called "H Blocks" of the Maze Prison near Belfast (from the air the building complexes look like a series of large Hs) a group of republican prisoners is on hunger-strike. They have all been tried and sentenced for violent offences, including murder. In the eyes of the Protestant community they are ordinary criminals. From their own point of view, however, and that of their supporters, they are soldiers, prisoners of war, meriting special treatment. So they refuse to wear prison clothes, and begin a series of protests — the "blanket" protest, when they refuse to wear any clothes except a blanket; and the "dirty" protest, when they refuse to clean out their cells, and for weeks live in the squalor of cells whose walls and ceilings are daubed with their own excrement. And then they go on hunger-strike "to the death". Ten of them die, including Bobby Sands, who has, while in jail, been elected to a seat in the Westminster parliament. Are they national heroes, giving their lives under a regime of political oppression? Or are they simply criminals, whose sufferings under detention are self-inflicted and avoidable? A divided community gives different answers. Black flags in the streets in one area show sympathy, while in another area an inscription on a gable-wall proclaims: "Let them die!"

* * *

At Darkley, in south county Armagh, there is a gospel hall, of a type common in Northern Ireland, where many Protestants belong to small groups of evangelical "brethren" or charismatic Christians. As the service is about to commence on Sunday, 21 November 1983, a shocked congregation watch as gunmen come in and spray the building with machine-gun fire, killing three elders of the congregation and wounding seven other members. The worshippers are people known to keep aloof from politics: this is what is known in Ireland as a "sectarian" murder, that is, killing people for no other reason than that they are Catholic or Protestant.

* * *

Sectarian murders are followed by other sectarian murders — on the other side. A Catholic petrol-pump attendant, a Protestant school-bus driver, both unconnected with the security forces or the paramilitary groups, are shot for no apparent reason. And after each death comes a funeral. Funerals have always taken a prominent part in Irish life, both Catholic and Protestant. And the funerals of those killed in the violence almost inevitably become occasions for the display of the grief and protest of one section of the community. Leading political figures will make a point of attending...

* * *

Sunday, 8 November 1987, was Remembrance Sunday, when all over Britain and Northern Ireland, and even in Dublin, ceremonies are held to recall the memory of those who died in the first and second world wars. In the town of Enniskillen the crowds are beginning to gather around the war memorial, when an IRA bomb, concealed in a building close by, explodes, killing eleven civilians, including women and children. It was meant, say the bombers, for the policemen and soldiers who might also have been there... One of the victims is a nineteen year-old nurse, buried under the rubble with her father, Gordon Wilson. As they hold each other's hands, she says: "Daddy, I love you very much." She dies, he survives... He has no words of condemnation for the killers, only forgiveness.

* * *

"The Birmingham Six" are six men jailed in 1974 for bomb attacks on two public houses in Birmingham, England, in which 21 people died. Shortly after the bombings they were arrested, tried, sentenced and jailed for life. But were they really guilty? They have always maintained their innocence. In 1987, an official inquiry was instituted: had the natural eagerness to find the perpetrators of an outrage led to a miscarriage of justice? The finding of the inquiry in January 1988 upheld the original judgment. But the doubts in people's minds were not allayed.

* * *

How *can* justice operate in a situation like Northern Ireland, however good the intention? Trial by jury is impossible, because witnesses are liable to intimidation. So there are one-judge courts (known as "Diplock" courts from the name of Lord Justice Diplock who first suggested them) which can judge on the basis of the uncorroborated evidence of a single informer or "supergrass". A travesty of justice? The best that can be done under the circumstances? The only practical alternative to long periods of detention without trial?

* * *

"Plastic bullets" are small baton-like missiles fired from special guns as an effective means of crowd-control. They have undoubtedly taken a number of lives, and caused numerous injuries. Yet how are police to defend themselves against attacks by petrol-bombs and even gunfire? Isn't it a better method than the *real* bullets which are used in so many countries?

* * *

Strip-searching. Since 1982 women prisoners in Northern Ireland — most of them awaiting trial — are not infrequently subjected to strip-searching, allegedly in order to prevent them carrying weapons or messages into or out of prison. The searches are carried out by women prison staff, but are experienced as humiliating and degrading. The fact that most of those searched belong to the minority (Catholic) community, and that such searches are much more frequent in Northern Ireland than in the Republic or Britain, where they also happen, makes the issue a deeply-felt one.

* * *

Flags fly everywhere in Northern Ireland. They announce the allegiance of the house or building where they fly — Union Jack or Ulster flag for the unionists (Protestant), and the green, white and orange tricolour for the nationalists (Catholic). But flags are not enough. In many unionist areas the kerb-stones are painted red, white and blue. And in nationalist areas the regulation red post-boxes and telephone booths are often over-painted in green. Colour counts.

On gable-walls there are paintings: King William III, Prince of Orange, riding his white horse at the 1690 battle of the Boyne for unionists, and a variety of motifs for nationalists, sometimes linking the deaths of the hunger-strikers with the death of Christ; blood as the price of liberation.

Around 12 July, which commemorates the Boyne, there will be Orange arches in unionist streets — elaborate constructions decorated with loyalist slogans, pictures of King William, and emblems of the Orange Order. This is the famous "marching season", when processions, nationalist as well as unionist, are taken along "traditional routes", which for Orangemen has often meant through nationalist areas.

* * *

There are typical *sounds* too. On warm summer evenings the distant rumblings of the great Lambeg drums, which on the day of the march are beaten till the blood runs from the drummer's knuckles. With the drums go the flute bands, and the massive painted banners, as the men march in their bowler hats, orange sashes and white gloves. For many Protestants, accustomed to church services of Puritan simplicity, the colour and music and excitement of the march provide an ingredient which is lacking in their normal diet of worship. There are nationalist occasions too, with pipe-bands, and banners with inscriptions in the Irish language.

And with the bands — the songs. On both sides these are unashamedly sectarian, recalling past victories and defeats, suffering and death. On the nationalist side especially the repertoire is constantly being augumented, as new heroes like Bobby Sands are added to the list; and on record, tape, video, and in "singing pubs" the music perpetuates and reinforces the political theme. On the unionist side — perhaps because of uneasiness about the distinctive Irishness of the music which underlies all Irish political songs, Catholic or Protestant — there are fewer songs; but the old ones retain their popularity.

* * *

Images of a divided community. And, especially in the cities and towns, the presence of the police and army will from time to time make itself obvious, with armed soldiers running down the street, taking up their positions in doorways, or driving past in armoured Land Rovers, green for the army, grey for the police. To the nationalist community, this presence of the security forces is oppressive: they feel it is directed against them, that the uniforms are symbols of a country which is not theirs, that there is a "shoot-to-kill" policy directed against them. To the loyalists, on the other hand, the security seems inadequate; they feel unprotected, and think of the unexpected bomb, the gunman at the hall-door, the car which may blow up as it is driven out of the garage.

And for both communities, the endlessly worsening unemployment. The nationalist community has suffered most, the unemployment rate there being twice as high as among Protestants; but now, as one after another the multinational companies close their operations in Northern Ireland, the Protestant working-class is similarly affected. More than 22 percent of all employees are out of work, and in some areas, like Strabane, the rate is far higher — more than 50 percent. Northern Ireland is the most disadvantaged part of the United Kingdom. What are young people to do? A Belfast teenager writes:

> God no, please!
> give me violence
> again, to drown this silence
> which is killing me
> … Big streets empty, full of little
> papers, cigarette ends, decaying spittle
> and walking here causes only the dust
> to move. [1]

---

[1] Quoted in Ray Davey, *Take Away This Hate*, Belfast, Corrymeela Press, n.d., p.119.

* * *

Yet the violence needs to be seen in perspective. At its worst, the casualties from political violence have never equalled in number those from road accidents. People who live in Northern Ireland smile when they hear of overseas visitors who come to Ireland but don't visit the North because it's too dangerous. They know that the chances of suffering violence are considerably less in Belfast — with a very low rate, for example, of drug-related crime — than in New York or even Dublin. Some sections of the community, however, have suffered a much higher incidence of violence than others, for example urban Catholics of the lowest income groups, and Protestant farmers living along the border between the Republic and Northern Ireland. All violence is deplorable, especially avoidable political violence. But it needs to be remembered that violence has many origins; that there are many more violent cities than Belfast; and that the great majority of men, women and children in Northern Ireland go about their life in much the same way as people anywhere else.

2. Land of Saints and Scholars

How Christian is Ireland? There can be few, if any, countries in the world where the level of church observance, both Catholic and Protestant, is so high. And the Christian tradition in Ireland goes back to very early times: it has, indeed, merited its title of "the land of saints and scholars".

The great missionary apostle of Ireland was the fifth-century St Patrick (himself a native of the larger island off Ireland's eastern coast). The church which he established had its ecclesiastical capital at Armagh, and churches and monasteries of the distinctive Celtic tradition soon spread all over the island. The great Irish monastic schools became famous throughout Christendom for their learning and missionary zeal, and it was largely through them that the Christian faith was re-established in a Europe which had been over-run by pagan barbarians. St Columba of Derry (521-97 AD) established a monastery on the Scottish island of Iona, and brought Christianity to the Pictish people. He was followed by great numbers of Irish missionaries who re-evangelized large tracts of Europe, establishing their monasteries in places as far away as St Gallen in Switzerland and Bobbio in Italy. The most famous of these Irish "pilgrims for Christ" in continental Europe was St Columbanus (d.615).

The visible signs of the Celtic church are still impressive. Not for them great Romanesque or Gothic cathedrals, for the Celtic church's buildings were small-scale and — with a few notable exceptions like the Gallarus Oratory on the Dingle Peninsula or the old stone churches in Kells and Glendalough — built of wood and earth. But they left beautifully carved stone high crosses (Monasterboice, Clonmacnoise), with elaborate panels depicting scenes from scripture. And their biblical manuscripts, adorned with the same interlaced Celtic motifs which decorate the crosses, but on a minute scale and brightened by glorious colours, are perhaps the most beautiful visible form which the written word of God has ever taken. Monks wrote the manuscripts between the sixth and eighth centuries and the most famous of all is the Book of Kells, which is treasured in the library of Trinity College Dublin.

The Celtic church also produced great Christian hymns, some of which, in translation, are sung all over the world, like "I bind unto myself today the strong Name of the Trinity" (attributed to St Patrick, but probably later), and "Be Thou my vision, O Lord of my heart". Not only Ireland, but a large part of Britain and of continental Europe is indebted for its evangelization to these missionary pilgrims of the Celtic church.

In later centuries Irish laymen and women — often emigrants or even refugees because of their faith or their politics — took their religious traditions with them wherever they went. One of the largest such migrations occurred in the late seventeenth and eighteenth centuries when many thousands of Irish Presbyterians emigrated to North America (the so-called "Scotch Irish" or "Ulster Scots"), and took a leading part in the events surrounding the founding of the United States in 1776. In the following century they were followed by another great wave of Irish emigrants, this time mostly Irish Catholics leaving an Ireland impoverished by the terrible famine of 1845-50. Catholic and Protestant Irish men and women played a leading part also in Australia in the period following the arrival of the "first fleet" in Sydney (1788).

From the ninth century, however, which marked the concluding stages of the great missionary movement of the Celtic church, the Irish churches as such played little part in world missions until the early nineteenth century. The reason was that for most of this period Ireland was subject to successive waves of conquerors and settlers, and the church had to concentrate its energies on survival. After the Reformation the Roman Catholic Church was under severe repression, Irish Catholic clergy were trained on the continent of Europe, and Ireland was itself regarded as a mission land. Only in the nineteenth century did the situation change, and in 1830 a short-lived mission went from Maynooth to India. The great development of Irish Catholic missions came in the closing decades of the nineteenth century after the religious orders — banished for most of the eighteenth century — had been re-admitted to Ireland and had built up their strength. Many thousands of members of the orders — men and women — went overseas to evangelize, educate and heal.

The Irish Protestant churches were in the field some decades earlier, and from the first took a leading part in the great missionary movement of the nineteenth and twentieth centuries. Missionaries from the Church of Ireland (Anglican), the Presbyterian Church and the Methodist Church went in large numbers to India, China and Africa. Later many others went from small interdenominational groups, both evangelical and charismatic, and the list of missionary martyrs of the Irish church — Catholic and Protestant — still grows each year.

Nor should it be thought that these wandering sons and daughters of Ireland were narrow-minded, bigoted people. From among their number came many leaders of missionary and ecumenical thought: people like Thomas and Alexander Campbell, founders of the Disciples Church in the USA; Amy Wilson Carmichael, pioneer of women's liberation in India; Tissington Tatlow of the Student Christian Movement; Charles Ranson of the International Missionary Council; ecumenical theologians like the twin brothers Anthony and Richard Hanson; Henry McAdoo, chairman of the first Anglican/Roman Catholic International Commission (ARCIC I); pioneering architects of the great new united churches like Donald Kennedy of the Church of North India and Davis McCaughey of the Uniting Church in Australia.

Some of the most familiar hymns, sung daily by English-speaking people all over the world, came from Irish writers. Mrs Frances Alexander's simplicity and directness are seen in "Once in royal David's city", "There is a green hill far away", and "All things bright and beautiful"; and from Henry Francis Lyte came "Praise, my soul, the King of heaven" and "Abide with me". In more modern days there have been writers and spiritual pioneers to enrich the Christian imagination and understanding of their generation — like Helen Waddell, Presbyterian interpreter of medieval mysticism; C.S. Lewis, author of *The Screwtape Letters* and the Narnia novels; John Main OSB, who has helped Christians of many churches towards a deeper spiritual life drawing on Indian methods of meditation.

In recent years Catholic missionaries and overseas clergy have been particularly notable for involvement in movements for justice and peace in a variety of countries, especially Latin America, the Philippines and South Africa. The witness against racism of Archbishop Hurley in South Africa and Bishop Donal Lamont in Zimbabwe is well known, as is the imprisonment of Fr Niall O'Brien in the Philippines.

In the famine crisis in Ethiopia in 1986 it was remarkable how often the on-the-spot person interviewed by international media turned out to be an Irish lay volunteer, sister or priest, working with *Trocaire* or *Concern*, two leading Irish Catholic relief organizations. And it was perhaps no accident that the moving spirit behind the massive response to that crisis provided by Band Aid and later Live Aid was Bob Geldof, an Irish Roman Catholic — albeit a far from orthodox one — from Dublin. The response per capita to that appeal was higher in Ireland (by no means a wealthy country by American or European standards) than anywhere else in the world. Irish people, Catholic and Protestant, are generous by nature, and are prepared to respond to human need, and to the cry for justice. They do not, however, find it any easier than anyone else to respond to the call for reconciliation, forgiveness and peace when it involves a perceived threat to their own way of life.

3. Who are we?

Let us listen to the voices of some typical women and men from different parts of Ireland as they sketch their outlook, and their "memories".

"I am a Roman Catholic from Dublin... I am proud of being a citizen of the Republic of Ireland, and identify fully with my country's long struggle for independence. I would like to see a united Ireland, but have no wish to achieve that by violence, especially without the consent of Northern Irish women and men who think differently from me. I have a number of Protestant friends (perhaps I would have fewer if I did not belong to the middle-class professional group), and find them not so different from myself, though on certain issues of family ethics like divorce, contraception and abortion their attitude is marginally less conservative than my own. I enjoy the ecumenical services we have in Unity Week each January. I know very little about Northern Ireland and am a bit afraid of going there: Northern people — both Catholic and Protestant — seem somehow different from us. I only wish people up there were less bigoted and more tolerant — like us here in Dublin."

"I am a Presbyterian from Belfast... I have nothing personal against Roman Catholics, but I believe that Luther and Calvin in the sixteenth century were right to challenge many Catholic beliefs and practices, and that even today it is necessary for Protestants to bear witness to biblical truth against the non-biblical beliefs and practices which are still to be found in the Catholic Church, in spite of the reforms of Vatican II. I know that many ministers and lay people in the Presbyterian Church are keen on the ecumenical movement, but I am not: I am afraid that it could ultimately lead to the re-absorption of the Protestant churches by Rome, and so I am glad that in 1979 the Irish Presbyterian Church withdrew from the World Council of Churches. Yes, I belong to the Orange Order and to the Official Unionist Party. I believe that if Ulster Protestants do not protect their own interests, then nobody else will; and as there is still a unionist majority in Northern Ireland I believe that political power should rest in unionist hands, and not be shared with people who reject Northern Ireland's right to exist as a separate political entity. I respect Roman Catholics, and I have Roman Catholic friends, but I don't think it's right to share in worship with them, because by doing that we are compromising our

principles, and implying that biblical truth is not essential to the Christian faith. I would like us to have friendly relations with the Irish Republic; but that means that they must be friendly to us, and give up their aggressive claims on our territory. We Protestants have something special to contribute to Ireland, and we shall never yield to coercion. 'No Surrender' was the motto of the defenders of Londonderry in the siege of 1689, and it is still our motto today."

"I am a Roman Catholic from Derry... Not *Londonderry*, by the way, for the 'London', added in the seventeenth century to the ancient Irish name of St Columba's home, is a symbol of wrongful British occupation of Irish territory. We Catholics of Derry — and especially of areas like the Bogside and the Creggan — have an unhappy history behind us, a history of being second-class citizens in our own city. Things are better now, but for years the odds were stacked against us by a system of 'gerrymandering' which gave power in local government to the Protestant minority when it should have belonged to the Catholic majority. That kept us out of jobs and out of decent housing. And we have suffered often from oppression by the police and the army in house-to-house searches and interrogations. We remember especially 'Bloody Sunday' in January 1972, when thirteen unarmed people were shot dead by the British army in typical over-reaction to a street disturbance.

"How could we support any political party which did not have a united Ireland as its aim? My own preference is for John Hume's SDLP (Social Democratic and Labour Party); but I can understand those who say that constitutional methods will get you nowhere, and that the violence of Sinn Fein and the provisional IRA is the only real option.

"My church supports ecumenism, and I am happy to go with it, but I don't see very much response on the Protestant side here in Derry. Still, there are some clergy and lay people who are prepared to cross barriers of distrust, and I am glad to cooperate with them. If only all the people of Derry could come together to fight the real enemies — unemployment and social deprivation — things would be very different."

"I am from the Church of Ireland (Anglican) in Enniskillen... We Protestants in the border areas of Fermanagh and Tyrone have suffered a great deal in the past twenty years. The town of

Enniskillen has been bad enough, but I think especially of people living in isolated farms near the border. So many men have been murdered there in sectarian attack that we don't hesitate to use the word 'genocide'. The sons and heirs of farmers are ambushed and shot on their tractors and in their homes, so that the land passes into Catholic hands. We feel that no one wants to protect us: the British government has taken out of our hands the power to protect ourselves, and it is easy for terrorists to escape across the border after their attacks. All we ask is freedom to live, and to go on being at peace with our neighbours. We belong here; and though my own ancestors came to Ireland from England in the early seventeenth century, the church they came to — the Church of Ireland — was already Anglican, since many of the bishops and clergy had accepted the Reformation. Our church has a continuous history going back to St Patrick, and we belong here and not anywhere else."

"I am a Methodist from Cork... I think our Protestant friends and relations in the North find it hard to believe that we Southern Protestants are perfectly happy down here, and able to take a full and acceptable part in the wider community. Our relations with our Roman Catholic neighbours are very good, and our ministers and church leaders are treated with respect and understanding by the leaders — church and civil — of the majority community.

"It's true that there are some pressures and problems. Our numbers continue to decline, and every now and again some little church has to be closed. Young people find better employment prospects elsewhere, perhaps in England. And interchurch marriages are a real problem; more than half of our young people marry Roman Catholics, and frequently, though by no means always, the children end up becoming Catholics. Education is also a difficulty. Our children either go to Protestant boarding schools (which is expensive, even though well supported by government), or else to local schools where most of their friends belong to the majority community.

"There are also some real problems in the area of family ethics — especially concerning divorce, contraception and abortion — where we feel that the law of the state reflects too closely the ethical teaching of the Roman Catholic Church. Remember that Irish Protestants on the whole take a conservative view of these matters, and by no means want a society where divorce is near normal and abortion can be had on demand. But most Irish Protestant parents — and many Catholics — believe that responsible parenthood is helped, not hindered, by contraception, and are glad that the law is now more relaxed on this matter than it was. They also believe that there are certain circumstances where, in order to save the mother's life in childbirth, abortion should be permitted; for that reason they have hestitations about using Catholic maternity hospitals. With regard to divorce: what do you do when a marriage really breaks down, and becomes 'dead'? Marriage breakdown is just as common in the Republic as in Northern Ireland (where divorce is legal), but here the situation is much more 'messy', because second relationships are sometimes formed and children are born who have no legal standing. Each church has, of course, a right to demand from its members the observance of its own standards. Yet in most countries in the world divorce is accepted as a basic human right — undesirable indeed, yet sometimes necessary in the interests of a better quality of life.

"I think I represent the attitude of most Protestants in the Republic. We accept the situation, despite its problems, and are happy to give our loyalty to this state. We believe that any difficulties we face can be resolved from within the Republic, and are glad to take our place within that developing society."

* * *

Those are fairly typical voices from the four "mainline" churches. But other, and much more strident, voices can be heard on both sides. A voice from the Rev. Ian Paisley's *Free Presbyterian Church* would say something like this:

"Your Cork Protestant gives the show away. These people have lived so long in the South that they have lost their moral fibre, their pride in being different, their desire to witness to the evangelical faith and to pass it on to their Catholic neighbours. They are prepared to live happily in a Catholic-dominated society, a society which has been wrecked by drink, gambling, dishonesty, Sabbath-breaking and slovenliness.

"Our problem with the South — and with our Catholic neighbours in the North — is not primarily political: it is religious. We see what the effect of that church has been on Irish people, South and North, and we don't like it. God has set us Protestants here in this country to witness to biblical truth, and we believe that our freedom to do so would be curtailed in an all-Ireland Republic dominated by the Catholic Church. We are afraid of that church: and we are determined to resist — if necessary by force — any attempt to coerce us to accept the kind of life-style it supports. We see ourselves as true 'defenders of the faith' — the Reformed faith — at a time when that faith is under attack not only from the Roman Catholic Church, its traditional opponent, but also from well-meaning but mistaken liberal, ecumenical Christians who do not realize that they are playing into the hands of a still-expansionist Roman Church. In Northern Ireland — and indeed all over the world — the Reformation is under attack, and we see ourselves as its front-line defenders."

* * *

And a voice from the *Sinn Fein Party* (the political wing of the *Provisional IRA*) would be very clear in its objectives:

"Our primary aim is to eliminate British power from Ireland. We have nothing against Protestantism as such, but if Irish Protestants identify themselves with the British, wear British uniforms and serve the British government, then they must suffer the consequences, for they become legitimate targets in the struggle for Irish independence. None of the churches, not even the Roman Catholic Church, seems to realize that this is a battle for liberation. We fail to see why theologians who give active support to the struggle for liberation in South Africa and in Latin America do not throw in their weight behind us. The ballot-box has got us nowhere in this battle: that is why we are prepared to use the armalite rifle and the bomb. Institutional violence such as our people have endured from the police and the army for years will yield only to violence; and so we are determined to continue the armed struggle until the British make a clear commitment to leaving Ireland."

4. "We're Different" — Images of Irish Church Life

People call it "Holy Ireland". Why?

Irish Catholic churches, especially in cities and towns, are very large buildings. And on Sunday mornings they are crowded, with one mass following another in quick succession: huge and crowded car-parks, and the streets filled with people coming and going. Figures as high as 90 percent of the population are claimed for weekly mass-attendance. Others believe that — especially among young people and in new housing areas — the figure is much lower. But it is still very high, perhaps 80 percent overall. It is still the accepted thing to go to church, and most people would feel very uncomfortable if they did not fulfill their mass obligation.

Apart from Sunday mass, however, most Catholics are not greatly involved in church activities. Christian education is left to the Catholic schools. Irish Protestants, largely because of cultural conditioning which has made many of them think in terms of "the blasphemy of the mass" (language of the polemical Reformation era still surviving), find it difficult to understand the centrality of the mass in the spiritual life of Catholics, for whom it is the place and the occasion where they regularly meet their Lord and renew their relationship with him.

Once Sunday mass is over — you're on holiday! So Sunday is the day for games, including major sporting events, especially in Gaelic football and hurling (the Irish equivalent of hockey). It's the day for parties and picnics, for the concert, for the cinema and for all kinds of celebrations.

Sunday in Belfast is very different from Sunday in Dublin. Virtually everything that can be closed is closed. It is the Lord's Day, the Christian Sabbath; and the fourth commandment is extended to prohibit not only work, but even play. In some Belfast parks the children's swings are chained up, in case any Sabbath-breaking children should wish to use them.

In many Protestant homes — like the one where I myself grew up — Sunday is *not* an irksome day. There are plenty of things to do, including church services and Sunday school: books to read, friends to meet, walks to enjoy; church activities like youth fellowship meetings. But the pressure towards rigid Sabbatarianism is there, and has its effect on both communities — just as the pressure in the South is towards a relaxed "continental Sunday".

In both these "Sunday" situations, some groups feel threatened. Many Protestant families in the South have agonized over whether or not the children should be allowed to play in competitive sports on Sundays. If they do, they miss going to church; if they don't, they miss a good opportunity of mixing normally with "the other side". How to decide? And in the North, Catholics — while they go ahead with their own sports fixtures — feel oppressed since so many places of entertainment are closed to them because of the wishes of the other community. The day of rest becomes a source of friction.

Patterns of spirituality

Ireland can show many different patterns of popular spirituality — perhaps "piety" would be a better word — both Catholic and Protestant. Let us look at two of them, one from each side.

The mission-tent. For many decades, and especially since the mid-nineteenth century renewal movement known as "the '59 Revival", Ulster Protestants have flourished on regular injections of evangelical Christianity through "missions" held in anything from a small marquee to a great auditorium like the King's Hall in Belfast. The speaker may be a little-known evangelist, or he may be Dr Billy Graham; but the emphasis is on preaching leading to personal conviction of sin, repentance and conversion. People are encouraged to believe that the *only* valid way of relating to God is through an evangelical conversion experience leading to a deep and explicit individual relationship with Christ. It is helpful if one can indicate the date and time when one's conversion took place.

There is nothing here that is different from similar movements in the United States or in Britain: indeed many of the speakers, the songs, the vocabulary, the techniques come directly from America. The result of the process is that people are divided into two groups: those who are "born-again Christians" and those who are not. The latter group is held to include not only all Roman Catholics, but also all ecumenical Protestants, as well, of course, as "nominal" Protestants. A common question is, "Are you a Christian?" And it is notoriously difficult to satisfy the questioner unless you can describe a conversion experience in acceptable evangelical terminology.

Lough Derg. Roman Catholics have their missions too, for example those traditionally carried out by the Redemptorist Fathers in country parishes. These are occasions when great crowds of parishioners will gather to hear a preacher urging them to deeper devotion, truer repentance, and a more Christian daily life. One of the most interesting examples of Irish Catholic piety is the annual penitential pilgrimage to Lough Derg in County Donegal, "St Patrick's Purgatory". This is an extremely tough ordeal for the thousands of people, young and old, who undertake it. More than 36 hours' stay under spartan conditions on an island in the middle of a cold lake, little sleep, black tea and dry toast, and long penitential walks around the rough stony "beds" in bare feet. And the result? Even sceptical participants speak of the purification, the sense of unity with centuries of penitent Christians seeking cleansing from sin... The penitential theme runs very deep in Irish spirituality.

Irish Catholics find it difficult to empathize with the mission-tent conversion experience, and feel hurt and excluded when, as so often happens, Protestants refuse to grant them the name of Christian, on the ground that they have never entered into an acknowledged and explicit personal relationship with Christ. And Protestants find it equally hard to empathize with the Lough Derg experience, which to them seems to be a classical example of "justification by works". To Catholics, much of Protestantism seems to be mere "fideism" — the exaltation of psychological "faith" into a justifying work. And Protestants see Catholic spirituality as being a matter of "works", of penance, of a sacramentalism which relies on the *ex opere operato* efficacy of a rite or duty rather than as a personal commitment to God in Christ.

The two spiritualities are felt to exclude each other.

Apartheid — Irish style

Today a definite form of apartheid operates in Northern Ireland, separating the Protestant and Catholic communities from each other. It is by no means a total apartheid: there are many individuals and groups on both sides who are opposed to it, and there are whole areas of society where it does not operate, especially in middle-class, professional and academic life. Nor is it an apartheid imposed by the state, since government policy in education, for example, has simply accepted an already existing tendency towards separatism. The Ulster version of apartheid means that over a wide area of society there is little or no social contact between the two communities. They live in separate areas, go to separate churches, attend separate schools, play different games, and finally are buried in separate cemeteries.

It was not always so. In the late eighteenth century, for example, when Presbyterians suffered under some of the same political and social disabilities as Catholics, members of these two churches joined hands in the United Irishmen movement and in the uprising of 1798. When St Patrick's Roman Catholic Church was built in Belfast in 1815, Protestant friends provided a substantial proportion of the money required. During the nineteenth century, however, a gulf between the two sides became slowly wider. The Catholic Church gradually developed its own independent school system (as it did in many other countries). As a result of this, the state education system in Northern Ireland (after 1920) became, unintentionally, a virtually all-Protestant affair, and almost the entire Catholic population went to Catholic schools. In the South of Ireland, where the state system was *de facto* operated largely by Catholics for Catholics, it was the Protestants who sought for separate educational facilities, where their children could be brought up in an atmosphere reflecting the Protestant outlook. As a result, most Irish children grow up — and for two generations at least have grown up — in isolation from children of the other community. Yet there have always been exceptions, and today there is a noteworthy movement towards "integrated" education.

Above school level there *are* chances to meet with the other community — at technical school, at university, in the work place. But by that time, attitudes and patterns of behaviour have often become fixed, and most people find it easier to stay within the bounds of their own group.

The difference extends even to games. In the North, Gaelic football and hurling are the Catholic games, and rugby the middle-class Protestant one, with association football providing a certain common ground. In the South the same rule applies, with the modification that rugby is now widely accepted in middle-class Catholic circles. On the whole, however, games do not provide the unifying force which they do in some other countries: even on television, you watch the bit of the programme which concerns *your* community, and switch off when "the others" come on.

As a result of this practical apartheid, people grow up with very little information about the other community, and such information as they do have is distorted. Some Protestants tend to assume that the Roman Catholic Church has not changed since the Reformation; some Catholics are surprised to learn that Protestants have sacraments and an ordained ministry, and affirm the Apostles' Creed. And there has developed the tendency to define one's own belief negatively, by saying what it is *not*. Protestants are people who do not believe in transubstantiation, in sacramental confession, in the papacy, in purgatory, in the Marian doctrines. Catholics do not believe in allowing the laity into the decision-making process, do not believe in the need for individual conversion, do not believe that gambling is a particularly bad thing. People judge each other's churches without ever seeking to understand them.

Slogans of separation

Ireland is good slogan country, and unlike in America, the graffiti are always legible. "No Surrender" is the great Protestant motto, going back to the siege of Protestants in Derry by King James II in 1689. In Catholic areas "Brits Out" is perhaps the most common message, and it is an uncomfortable one for Ulster Protestants, who regard themselves as British, but have no other country to go to, and indeed no intention of leaving. "You are now entering Free Derry" is a slogan which separates one part of that city from another. There are the "Remember" slogans: "Remember 1916" (the republican rising in Dublin at Easter 1916, and the proclamation of the Republic); "Remember 1690" (King William III's victory over James II at the Boyne). There are still many fading inscriptions recording the H-Block crisis and the death of Bobby Sands: "Smash H-Block", "Bobby Sands R.I.P." And besides the many uncomplimentary personal messages, directed either against the queen or against the pope, there is the omnipresent Protestant

message since the Anglo-Irish Agreement of 15 November 1985
— "Ulster Says No."

There have been martyr-figures on both sides. There are
many slogans of separation. There has not yet appeared the
great slogan of reconciliation which can unite hearts without
crushing people and identities.

* * *

We have used the word apartheid. But is the Ulster situation
really comparable to South Africa? There are many differences.

Colour is not involved. Though one does hear talk of ethnic
differences, yet in fact the Irish people, North and South, are a
very mixed lot, with Celtic, Norman and Anglo-Saxon traits
well and truly intermingled. And it has always been possible for
individuals to move from one group to the other, through
intermarriage, for example, or through religious — or political
— conversion.

It would also be difficult to maintain that Irish apartheid today
was imposed by the state. Such an attitude was present in the
former Unionist government at Stormont, one of whose leaders,
Lord Brookeborough, spoke of "a Protestant Parliament for a
Protestant people"; though indeed at that time many Catholics,
including church leaders, had no wish to recognize or cooperate
with the state, and maintained their own separateness. Historically the apartheid goes back to the incursion of large numbers
of foreign settlers into a country where previously they had no
place. The "settler" factor is the dominant one in Ireland, rather
than the racial one, and is compounded by the fact that the
seventeenth-century settlers were all Protestants while the original inhabitants were mainly Catholics. Today, however, the
apartheid operates mostly as a self-imposed distancing, which
large numbers of the population choose to maintain, and which
has been reinforced by the violence which began in 1968, in
which thousands of people were intimidated into leaving their
homes in mixed areas, and moving into the relatively safer
environment of a Catholic or Protestant ghetto. As a result, the
whole community is physically more polarized than it has ever
been before, and the number of places with mixed populations
has been heavily reduced.

There are, however, many areas, for example in some country districts and also in the middle-class suburbs of cities and towns, where people do live together in harmony. And there are many people from the more troubled areas who see it as their Christian witness to "break down the enmity" by establishing and maintaining close links with the other side.

5. The Background of "the Troubles"

There was no sixteenth-century Reformation in Ireland; no Irish Luther or Calvin or Knox or Cranmer. Protestantism therefore did not emerge as a spontaneous movement for reform within the Irish church, but was imposed from England by law as part of the Tudor monarchy's policy of "anglicizing" Ireland, in the reign of Henry VIII and Elizabeth I.[1] The ordinary people, and many of the clergy, did not accept the Reformed faith, which was regarded as a foreign importation, and associated with the suffering and destruction caused by the suppression of the clergy, together with the dissolution of the monasteries and the collection of taxes for a church to which the people owed no allegiance.

The sense of foreignness was compounded when, following the defeat of Hugh O'Neill's rebellion and the Flight of the Irish Earls in 1607, the lands of the great Irish chieftains were confiscated, and large numbers of settlers or "planters" were brought in — Anglicans from England and Presbyterians from Scotland — in the Ulster "Plantation" of James I. These early settlers, brought in by government policy, were later followed by others under free enterprise, so that all nine counties of the province of Ulster (including the three counties of Donegal, Cavan and Monaghan, which are not part of the modern political entity of Northern Ireland) received a substantial influx of Protestant settlers. Although the Earls had fled, most of the native Irish population remained, excluded from their ancient lands, and driven to seek a living on barren hill tracts, or as labourers on the farms and in the townships of the settlers.

Both communities had much to endure, and memories of oppression, persecution and resistance soon accumulated. The massacre of many Protestant settlers in 1641 (remembered especially in Portadown, where men, women and children were drowned in the River Bann) was followed by Cromwell's ferocious sack of Drogheda in 1649. Forty years later, in 1689, came the siege of Derry, when the Protestant defenders, surrounded by the armies of the Catholic King James II, held out for more than a hundred days until finally relief came when

---

[1] T.W. Moody, *The Ulster Question 1603-1973*, Dublin, Mercier Press, 1974, p.3.

the ship "Mountjoy" broke through the blockading boom across the river Foyle. In the following year, James was decisively defeated by William of Orange at the battle of the Boyne, and the Protestant succession to the British throne was confirmed. "Derry's walls and 'No Surrender'", and "the green grassy slopes of the Boyne" became symbolic watchwords of beleaguered Protestantism.

For most of the eighteenth century the Catholics lived under severe penal laws, unable to meet for mass in churches, and forced instead to gather at "mass rocks" in the open. Many priests were hunted down and killed, and the restrictions on ordinary Catholics — prevented from holding public office, owning any considerable property, even owning a good horse — made life in the "penal days" nasty, brutish and short. It is true that at times the Presbyterians (or Dissenters as they were called) suffered under similar restrictions, and even some additional ones (like being forbidden to celebrate marriages); but over the years it was certainly the Catholics who were treated as a subject people, without political rights, and despised for the poverty and squalor which had been forced upon them. Ninety-five percent of the land surface of Ireland passed into Protestant hands.

Things began to change for the better before the end of the eighteenth century, for example with the opening of St Patrick's College, Maynooth, a royal foundation of 1795, which became a great centre for the training of the Irish Catholic priesthood. But not until 1829 did the British parliament pass the act for Catholic Emancipation, which enabled Catholics to be elected to parliament. The Catholic Relief Act of Grattan's Dublin parliament of the 1780s had already given the vote to some of the Catholic middle class.

The closing decade of the eighteenth century was one which brought some Protestants and Catholics closer together than ever before, largely through the spread of Enlightenment ideas like those which inspired the American Revolution of 1776, many of whose leaders were in fact Ulster Presbyterians who had left Ireland because of religious and political oppression. And the 1798 rising, like Robert Emmet's revolt in 1802, was in its beginnings largely inspired by Protestants who had the needs of the whole community at heart.

In the nineteenth century, however, the alienation between the two communities increased once more, as Catholic nationalism, under Daniel O'Connell, became more and more of a successful popular cause. There were changes in Protestant affiliations also. In the eighteenth century Presbyterians in the North had been a disadvantaged group, suffering discrimination from the established Church of Ireland and from government, and as a result often allying themselves with their even more oppressed Catholic fellow-citizens. As O'Connell's popularity increased, and with it the self-consciousness of Ireland as a Gaelic, Catholic nation, so Presbyterians, under the leadership of the orthodox and anti-Enlightenment Henry Cooke, tended to ally themselves more and more with the Establishment, thus preparing the way for the eventual emergence of the Unionist Party, dedicated to maintaining the union between Britain and Ireland.

The last decade of the nineteenth century saw a largely Protestant initiative in the beginnings of the "Gaelic Revival", a movement to restore the Irish language, which was in imminent danger of disappearing, and to develop the national consciousness of the Gaelic heritage in literature, art and music. Writers like W.B. Yeats, Douglas Hyde and J.M. Synge were its early leaders, but gradually it became more political, especially under the influence of Patrick Pearse. It was a process not unlike that which was happening simultaneously in India under the violence-orientated Bal Gangadhar Tilak, except that in Ireland no Gandhi arose to show that non-violent nationalism can be more effective than violent. Pearse and his companions in the leadership of the 1916 Easter Rising were executed, but not before they had proclaimed the Republic from the steps of the General Post Office in Dublin. Five years later, after the end of the 1914-18 war and the bitter war of independence (1919-21), Britain conceded the Irish demand for "Home Rule", and the Irish Free State came into being, predecessor of the present Republic of Ireland. The price of independence was partition, and by the Government of Ireland Act of 1920 six counties of the old nine-county province of Ulster remained part of the United Kingdom, under the name of Northern Ireland.

That political solution remained intact for almost fifty years, till the beginning of the present troubles in 1968. The South of

Ireland underwent a process of continuous political development, first as the Irish Free State, and later as the Republic of Ireland; first within and later outside the British Commonwealth, and eventually as a member of the European Community. Always, however, its political leaders made it clear that the struggle for independence remained incomplete as long as Northern Ireland remained British, and this claim was enshrined in Articles 2 and 3 of the Republic's 1937 Constitution.

Meantime Northern Ireland had its own parliament in the Belfast suburb of Stormont, but also sent MPs to Westminster. And at Stormont one party — the wholly Protestant Unionist Party — controlled the government uninterruptedly. The normal pattern of British or Irish party politics could not work, as voting was always on the Unionist/Nationalist pattern, and there was no possibility of the minority Catholic community ever achieving power.

The churches in the Stormont era

During the Stormont era, the Roman Catholic Church and the other churches maintained their distance from each other. As representatives of a people who did not accept the partition of the island, the Catholic bishops tended to ignore the government in public. At the same time they naturally did all they could to secure maximum benefits for their community in such fields as education and health. The State was there, and it was necessary to accept it, however reluctantly. But there was no incentive to support political structures in which one's community could never have any hope of playing an active role.

The Protestant churches were, naturally, much happier with the government, most of whose leaders were members of one or another of the churches. Not that the churches controlled the government; and indeed there were many issues where one or more of the churches found themselves in direct conflict with the government, for example over education. But the Union Jack — the British national flag symbolizing the union of England, Scotland and Ireland — often flew above or inside churches, and there was an easy assumption that this British-Ulster way of life must be the only norm for everyone in the province.

A parallel situation had developed in the Republic, and was seen particularly in the 1937 constitution, which, while recognizing the other main churches, gave a special place to the Roman Catholic Church (a provision eventually ended by a referendum in 1972). Protestant observers, particularly in the North, felt that the Roman Catholic hierarchy exercised much too great an influence in public life, for example in the celebrated case of Dr Noel Browne's "Mother and Child" health scheme of 1951, which had to be dropped on the insistence of the then Archbishop of Dublin, Dr McQuaid. The fact that the same archbishop made it a mortal sin for Catholics to attend Trinity College, Dublin, the famous Protestant foundation, did not go unremarked. Nor did the prohibition of divorce in the 1937 constitution.

The Orange Order

The Orange Order originated in 1796, at a time when other orders and brotherhoods were springing up in Britain, Ireland, Europe and America, frequently with an organization similar to that of Masonic Lodges. It was a Protestant defence organization, in the period immediately preceding the nationalist rising in 1798, and at first most of its members belonged to the Church of Ireland (Anglican). As its name implies, it sought to perpetuate the victory of William of Orange over James II.

During the nineteenth century the Order grew, and in many ways fulfilled the functions of a social club. The special celebration each year was on 12 July, when the 1690 Battle of the Boyne was recalled by local "marches", with banners, drums and fifes, and by meetings where patriotic (i.e. loyalist and pro-British), anti-Catholic and occasionally inflammatory speeches were made.

The Orange Order has never been an armed or a violent organization; its members traditionally parade in bowler hats, umbrellas and gloves, in addition to their orange sashes; and it is committed by its rules to a biblical Christianity, and to respect for those of other traditions, including Catholics. Its undoubted power, however, has stemmed from its political influence. Not to belong to the Order meant virtual exclusion from promotion in the Unionist Party. And if anyone had the courage to step out of line and advocate policies in conflict with the traditional ones, he could be sure of running into powerful opposition, as Captain Terence O'Neill found during the brief period when he sought *détente* (1963-69).

Although the Order is not a military organization, there is no doubt that over the years many of its members have in fact had access to weapons. During the Stormont era, this occurred through their membership of the RUC (the Royal Ulster Constabulary), and especially of the auxiliary police known as the B Specials. In more recent days, after the disbanding of the B Specials in 1969, the Ulster Defence Regiment (UDR) of the British Army has drawn its recruits mainly from the Protestant community. It is only natural that the Orange Order should provide an atmosphere which encourages young Protestant men and women to enter the security forces in defence of their homes and their liberty.

There are, as we shall see, several Protestant paramilitary bodies, such as the Ulster Volunteer Force (UVF) and Ulster Freedom Fighters (UFF), which operate violently and illegally. These have no organic relationship with the Orange Order, and emerged only after the political events of 1972.

The Irish Republican Army (IRA)

The antecedents of the IRA go back to the Irish Republican Brotherhood (IRB) of the nineteenth century. What is now called "the Old IRA" organized the Easter Rising in 1916, and proclaimed the Republic in Dublin. During the Stormont era the IRA remained quiescent for long periods, but from time to time, for example in 1939 and again in 1956, it organized bombing campaigns against British government and civilian targets in England and Northern Ireland. The IRA, distinguished as "Official" from the later Provisional IRA (see below p.32), developed a Marxist basis in its social analysis. It was illegal on both sides of the border, but had a considerable degree of support among the many nationalists who felt that the Irish government, despite its commitment to a united Ireland, was doing little to achieve its goal. The official wing of the IRA called a cease-fire in 1972, which has lasted ever since.

Opposing structures

There was, then, a complex array of power structures (including the churches) on both sides of the border at the beginning of the "Troubles" in 1968.

— The nationalist (Roman Catholic) population, South and North, was conscious of their historical continuity with the ancient language, culture and religion of the whole island.

— The Protestant population, while it could make a notable claim, through the Church of Ireland, to have an equal continuity, was yet conscious that the majority of its members had come to Ireland as colonists in the seventeenth century, displacing the original population. Yet they felt totally at home in a land which they had tamed, improved and made prosperous.

— On the nationalist side, the IRA was prepared to advance the cause of national unity by armed struggle. The government of the Southern State had the same goal of unity, but felt obliged to work for it *politically* and to conscientize its own population and the wider world by giving re-unification a high profile.

— The Northern Ireland government at Stormont (to which, up to 1968, the Westminster government had largely handed over responsibility for Ulster affairs) existed mainly in order to perpetuate the border, and the Protestant hegemony in Northern Ireland which that implied. It was able to respond directly to the threat of the IRA (and the more long-term threat of the political activity of the Southern government) by its armed police, who were able to keep the IRA's activities within strict limits.

— In all these efforts, Stormont could rely on the backing of the Orange Order, which ensured that unionism would continue to be supported by the vast majority of Protestant voters, so that not even the high unemployment of the 1930s Depression would persuade the Protestant working-class to throw in its lot with its Catholic fellow-workers.

That was the uneasy background against which the Irish churches had to operate when in 1968 the situation suddenly changed, and open violence began to escalate.

6. The Troubles

The 1960s were good times for many people in Ireland, which had at last begun to share in some of the increasing prosperity of the Western world at that time. Industrial development and international investment were happening in both North and South, and even the political climate had at last begun to thaw a little, under the prime ministership of Terence O'Neill in the North and Sean Lemass in the South, who in 1965 broke new ground by actually visiting each other and talking about cooperation.

There were, however, people on both sides of the religious divide who were determined that such cooperation should not develop. Right-wing unionists saw the thaw as a sign of Protestant weakness, which would ultimately lead to a republican take-over of Northern Ireland and a Roman take-over of Protestantism. Radical republicans did not want to see cooperation between two right-wing governments, one in the North and one in the South: they wanted to create the conditions under which an all-Ireland socialist republic would become a possibility.

Meantime, in 1967, a new factor had been added to the situation, largely under the influence of the American civil rights movement led by Martin Luther King and of radical student unrest in Europe. The Northern Ireland Civil Rights Association (NICRA), based largely on Queen's University in Belfast, began agitating for better housing, fairer allocation of houses and jobs, and an end to religious discrimination. At first the movement attracted support from both sides of the community, and idealistic Protestants and Catholics felt that they had found something to fight *for*, together.

Unfortunately the euphoria did not last. The reaction on the Protestant side was led by the Rev. Ian Paisley, a consistent opponent of the ecumenical movement. Paisley's own background was not Presbyterian but Baptist, his father being minister of a small independent Baptist church, in which Paisley himself was ordained. In the early 1950s he conducted a noisy campaign against what he denounced as Romeward trends in the Presbyterian Church. Trouble between a minister and his elders in a small country Presbyterian church gave him the opportunity to step in and found his own group, to which he gave the name of Free Presbyterian Church, with himself as moderator. Since then his church has grown, though by no means spectacularly, its membership being perhaps 15,000 against the Presbyterian Church's 350,000. The Free Presbyterian Church has, however, been a thorn in the flesh to the more liberal churches: hard-line elders or members of a Presbyterian church can threaten to leave and join Paisley if the minister does not produce the kind of conservative, anti-Catholic theology and politics which they want.

At the time of the civil rights movement, Paisley's immediate targets were the open display of the Irish tricolour flag, and the reforming prime minister of Northern Ireland, Terence O'Neill, whom he portrayed as a traitor to the Protestant cause. Partly in response to Paisley's opposition, the civil rights movement began to be infiltrated by radical republican supporters, some of them with links with the IRA. A more radical student organization, People's Democracy, was formed at Queen's University, and it was not long before violence erupted. The worst incident at this stage was the attack at Burntollet by Protestant "bully-boys" on a People's Democracy march from Belfast to Londonderry, in which the police did nothing to defend the marchers, and even joined their attackers (January 1969).

From that time until the present there has been a constant stream of violence and counter-violence in Northern Ireland, reaching its peak in 1972, when 474 people were killed. After nearly twenty years of violence the struggle still continues. We shall look at some of the main developments in the situation.

* * *

The events of the "marching season" in summer 1969 were critical. On 12 August the Protestant "Apprentice Boys" of Derry — so called in commemoration of the group of young apprentices who in the 1689 siege closed the gates of the city against King James II — marched into the Catholic Bogside area, where they came under attack. The police retaliated with violence, and on 14 August the British Army intervened between the two sides. On 16 August Protestants from the Shankill area in Belfast attacked Catholics in the Falls Road area. Again the police proved partisan, and the army was called in to restore peace. In the violence, six people were killed and 150 Catholic homes burnt. The large-scale violence had begun.

At this stage the nationalist population welcomed the British soldiers as their protectors. It was a role which did not last long.

Under the pressure of these events, the government of Northern Ireland passed several notable reforms between 1969 and 1972. The "rate-payer's franchise" was abolished. Local government electoral boundaries were revised, so eliminating "gerrymandering". The RUC was disarmed. And a Housing Executive was set up to ensure that the building and allocation of housing in the public sector was on a non-sectarian basis.

Meantime new political parties had been emerging. In 1970 the SDLP (Social Democratic and Labour Party) was formed bringing together constitutional nationalists in one strong group. The Alliance Party was founded as a means of uniting Catholics and Protestants, a role which it has carried out in exemplary, if small-scale, fashion. In September 1971 Ian Paisley formed the DUP (Democratic Unionist Party), in opposition to the continuing programme of reforms which the new Ulster premier, Brian Faulkner, was advocating.

After the events of August 1969 a group of Belfast members of the IRA, dissatisfied with their leaders' preference for Marxist political action, broke away and formed the Provisional IRA, soon to be known as the "Provos". In 1971 they killed their first British soldier, and gradually they built up a violent offensive, aimed at the breakdown of government. Brian Faulkner's government responded by introducing internment without trial, a measure which naturally caused great opposition and alienation in the Catholic community. There were demonstrations, after one of which — in Derry in January 1972 — British troops shot dead 13 unarmed people in the terrible incident which became known as "Bloody Sunday". Provisional IRA retaliation followed in Belfast on 21 July, "Bloody Friday", when 11 people were killed and 130 injured. The reaction of the British government under Edward Heath was to suspend the Northern Ireland parliament at Stormont and introduce "Direct Rule" from Westminster, with the aim of ensuring that acceptable British standards of justice operated in Northern Ireland.

The emergence of Protestant paramilitary groups dates from this period. During the violence of 1969 "vigilante" groups of volunteers had been formed in many streets to protect the inhabitants against the IRA, often by erecting barricades. The

UDA (Ulster Defence Association) arose out of these groups, and claimed many thousands of adherents. Although it was not an armed organization, many of its members did have access to weapons. Later other, more sinister groups appeared, notably the UFF (Ulster Freedom Fighters) and the UVF (Ulster Volunteer Force), which was made illegal by the government in 1975. As the years went on, Protestant paramilitary activity, in the form of sectarian murders, frequently parallelled that of the Provisional IRA.

With the arrival of William Whitelaw as the first Secretary of State for Northern Ireland, it was hoped that "devolved rule" could soon be restored, in a manner acceptable to the Catholic community. By now it had been realized that this could be done only by some system of "power-sharing", since otherwise the nationalists would never have access to power. Such a system was devised in 1973, with an assembly and a power-sharing executive, which took office on 1 January 1974, so bringing about — for the moment — the ending of Direct Rule. A tripartite conference had been held in December at Sunningdale (in England) between the Northern Ireland leaders of the executive, and ministers from the Republic and the United Kingdom. It was agreed that the new system should include an "Irish dimension", with a Council of Ireland composed of a consultative assembly and a council of ministers, each with equal representation from North and South.

The very hopeful Sunningdale experiment was short-lived. Paisley's DUP and other unionists formed a coalition to fight against power-sharing and the Irish dimension, and a new body, the Ulster Workers' Council, organized a general strike (15-29 May 1974), supported by Protestant paramilitaries. The unionist members of the executive resigned, Sunningdale collapsed, Direct Rule was resumed on 28 May, and has continued ever since.

The next significant series of events was focused on the treatment of those imprisoned for political violence. Internment without trial ended as a result of the Gardiner Committee report in 1975, and after that political prisoners were no longer given the "special category" status which William Whitelaw had introduced in 1972, but were treated as ordinary criminals under sentence. The Bennett Inquiry of 1976 faced the fact that police interrogations had often been brutal and degrading, and took steps to improve the situation. As a result, the police had to rely more and more on the evidence of informers, the so-called "super-grasses": under the Diplock system it was possible for a single judge to sentence prisoners on the uncorroborated evidence of an informer — a system which has inevitably come under heavy criticism.

The years 1980-81 saw the H-Block crisis (see above p.1). The "blanket" protest turned into the "dirty" protest, and that in turn into hunger-strikes, in which ten prisoners died. Although the European Commission on Human Rights eventually judged that the prisoners' sufferings had been self-inflicted, the episode marked a serious deterioration in relationships between the nationalist community (including members of the Roman Catholic hierarchy) on the one hand and the Ulster Protestant community and the British public on the other.

After the hunger-strikes, the Provisional IRA and its political wing, Sinn Fein, began to develop their specifically political activity, following their twin policy of "the armalite (rifle) and the ballot-paper". The Sinn Fein party rapidly became a force to be reckoned with, appearing, as it did, to be more capable of dealing effectively with nationalist grievances than the constitutional SDLP. In the 1983 British general election, Sinn Fein gained 15 percent of the Northern Ireland vote, as against 18 percent for the SDLP. There was a real possibility that the party of violence could take over as the main political representative of the nationalist community.

At this point a new initiative began to take shape, which was to have far-reaching effects, culminating in the Anglo-Irish Agreement of 15 November 1985. The process had begun in 1980 when the Irish Taoiseach (prime minister) Charles Haughey had agreed with Mrs Thatcher to set up a study process to consider "the totality of relationships within these islands". In 1981 the new Taoiseach, Garret FitzGerald, and Mrs Thatcher agreed to set up an Anglo-Irish intergovernmental council, at ministerial and official levels. A new and positive process of dialogue had commenced. In 1983, on the initiative of John Hume, a "forum" of the constitutional nationalist parties, North and South, was set up in Dublin, known as the New Ireland Forum, with the task of spelling out the kind of Ireland they hoped for in the future. Many individuals and groups, including Protestants, and even some Northern unionists, made contributions to the Forum, and perhaps the most interesting public session — fully televized — was that in which a delegation of the Irish Episcopal Conference of the Roman Catholic Church presented a report, and submitted to questioning by the politicians. The Forum report affirmed — for the first time in a nationalist document — the right of Northerners not only to be Protestant, but also to be British, so giving a quite new recognition to the Northern identity. It envisaged three possible solutions to the question of Northern Ireland: (1) a unitary state for the whole island, which was its preferred solution; (2) a federal Ireland; (3) joint authority. Mrs Thatcher rapidly made it clear that none of these three solutions was acceptable to her: "Out, out, out" was her response. Nevertheless, in the event the British and Irish governments *did* take the Forum seriously, and a process of discussion was instituted which proceeded without interruption until the signing of the Anglo-Irish Agreement at Hillsborough on 15 November 1985.

The Anglo-Irish Agreement

The Anglo-Irish Agreement is an internationally-registered agreement between the governments of the United Kingdom and of Ireland, seeking "to develop the unique relationship between their two peoples", to diminish divisions in Ireland and to achieve lasting peace and stability. It recognizes the rights of the two major traditions in Northern Ireland: the unionists who wish for no change in the present status of Northern Ireland, and the nationalists who "aspire to a sovereign united Ireland achieved by peaceful means and through agreement". It rejects violence, and recognizes the right of each community "to pursue its aspirations by peaceful and constitutional means" (preamble).

The Agreement affirms that any change in the status of Northern Ireland would come about only with the consent of a majority of the people of Northern Ireland. It recognizes that the present wish of the majority is for no change of status. And it declares that if in the future a majority should clearly *wish for* and consent to a united Ireland, the two governments would introduce the appropriate legislation (Art.1).

The machinery for carrying out the Agreement consists of an intergovernmental conference, which meets at both ministerial and official levels. And there is a secretariat, at present located in Belfast, to service the conference. The hope is expressed that certain responsibilities of the conference may eventually be devolved within Northern Ireland on a basis widely accepted in the community. Meantime the conference has powers to concern itself with many matters: the rights of the communities; human rights; discrimination; the use of flags and emblems; the desirability of a bill of rights. The Irish government is given power to put forward its views for proposals for major legislation in these areas, including questions relating to fair employment and to the police authority for Northern Ireland. So far as the security forces (especially the police) are concerned, special measures are to be taken to make them more acceptable to the nationalist community, and to increase the proportion of nationalist members in the force (Art.7). The conference can also make suggestions on the administration of justice (Art.8).

The Agreement is to come up for revision at the end of three years, i.e. by 15 November 1988.

Ulster says No

The Anglo-Irish Agreement was welcomed not only in Britain and in the Republic, but in international circles generally. It was, however, met by immediate and total rejection by the great majority of Protestants in the North. "Ulster Says No" became the slogan, and huge meetings were held in Belfast and Ballymena to protest. Local councils with Protestant majorities refused to function; the unionist MPs at Westminster resigned their seats en masse, and government ministers were ostracized.

What was the reason for this rejection? First, the fact that the unionists had not been included in the discussion leading to the Agreement, and that it had been reached over their heads, while the SDLP, and especially John Hume, had taken a leading part in its formulation. Secondly, it was felt that the secretariat in Belfast, which included civil servants from the Dublin government, was a "derogation from sovereignty": the Irish government was, the unionists said, helping to run Northern Ireland, and this they could never accept. Nothing that has happened since November 1985 has had any real effect on this attitude of total rejection: the unionists take the line that they will discuss no alternative system of government until the Anglo-Irish Agreement is abrogated.

The republican paramilitary movement — Provisional IRA/ Sinn Fein and INLA — also rejected the Agreement, for the diametrically opposite reason that it was seen as firmly entrenching British sovereignty, and moving away from the ideal of a united Ireland. And so the armed struggle has continued unabated. The unionists point to this continued violence, and argue that the Agreement, which was meant to create closer cooperation between the Northern and Southern security forces, has in fact done nothing of the kind: the violence is as bad as ever.

This is the situation of deadlock and alienation which the Irish churches have to face in 1988 and the future.

7. Breaking down the Enmity — Christian Responses

How have Christians responded to this situation? Let us look first at the responses of groups which are not officially appointed by the churches, and so have considerable freedom of action, expecially freedom to cross the Catholic/Protestant divide.

Unofficial groups

In Ireland, as in other countries, Protestant interchurch cooperation, especially in mission work overseas, had begun even before the Edinburgh Missionary Conference of 1910, and after that had developed quite considerably. But it was very unusual for effective contact to be made across the Roman Catholic/Protestant divide. Yet there had been some brave pioneering attempts in this direction, notably the work of the Mercier Society in Dublin in the 1930s and 40s, while in the 1950s there had been, in Ireland as elsewhere, considerable cooperation between Catholic and Protestant scholars in the fields of biblical studies, theology and liturgy. It was however, as a result of the Second Vatican Council (1962-65) that the climate really changed, and groups and organizations began to emerge with reconciliation and Christian unity as their primary purpose.

Early starters were two series of annual conferences for interchurch clergy and laity at Glenstal Abbey near Limerick (1964) and at Greenhills Presentation Convent, Drogheda (1966). These conferences provided, and still provide, an opportunity for organized but unofficial contact between Catholic and Protestant clergy and laity, and have done much to promote theological and liturgical discussion, and also to build friendship and confidence between leaders in the different churches. They have also had a catalytic effect, for example in creating a climate of opinion in which the later official Ballymascanlon meetings could develop, and also in specific initiations like the launching of *Irish Ecumenical News* (suggested at Glenstal 1981) and the formation of the Interchurch Group on Faith and Politics (Greenhills 1983).

Corrymeela is a place, a group of white buildings perched on a cliff at the extreme north-east corner of Ireland, looking across the sea towards Scotland. The Corrymeela Community, founded in 1965 by the Rev. Ray Davey, at that time Presbyterian chaplain at Queen's University, Belfast, is a mixed group — men and women,

Catholic and Protestant, lay and clerical — of about 150 members, who are united by a simple rule of life, and carry on a variety of careers in society. Corrymeela is a place where the most diverse groups and individuals come for peace, excitement, prayer and friendship: perhaps children from two schools — one Catholic and one Protestant — in Belfast; senior citizens, Catholic and Protestant together; politicians; policemen; students; clergy. In July every second year there is a week-long "Summerfest", reminiscent of a German Kirchentag, to which people of all ages come from Ireland and many other countries. Eventually everyone goes back home to their own particular situation, for "Corrymeela begins when you leave", as a notice at the gate proclaims.

A schoolgirl spent a few days at Corrymeela, mixing with children of the "other" community, attending prayers in the Croi (heart), the underground stone chapel at the centre of the place. Her verdict — "Corrymeela is a great place: there's no religion here" — was not a reflection on Corrymeela's inadequacy. It indicated the expectation of religion in which she had grown up, as something divisive, even violent: in Corrymeela she had found something different. So have thousands of others.[1]

The Cross Group is also different. On Sunday evening, 9 February 1975, Gerard Kiely, a 19 year-old first-year student at Queen's University, was shot as he was coming out of mass in a suburban Roman Catholic Church in Belfast. Two gunmen had waited as the people filed out, and fired indiscriminately into the crowd. Maura Kiely, Gerard's mother, nearly lost her faith. But Easter was coming, and she began to realize that God had chosen her to suffer, for a purpose. "I knew that if we were going to remain bitter we were going to destroy ourselves completely as a family." A priest said to her: "Why don't you start something?" So she went through newspaper files to find people who had suffered like herself, Catholic and Protestant. She did not write or phone: she visited each home personally.[2] The result was the emergence of the Cross Group — a group of people who had suffered the violent death of a close relative. They have been able to give each other understanding and support: their number, sadly, is still growing.

---

[1] Ray Davey, *Take Away This Hate*, Belfast, Corrymeela Press, n.d., p.116.
[2] Ray Davey, *An Unfinished Journey*, Belfast, Corrymeela Press, n.d.

The Irish School of Ecumenics, founded by Fr Michael Hurley SJ in 1970, was an interchurch response to the new openness between Christians which followed Vatican II. It provides a place for clergy, teachers and potential leaders of the different churches, from Ireland and from overseas, to meet in a community of serious study dedicated to the understanding and resolution of theological and other differences. Affiliated to Trinity College, Dublin, and to the University of Ulster, it supplies an academic basis in ecumenical studies in a context of shared koinonia and worship. As well as the School's regular courses of study it organizes interchurch conferences for clergy, laity and theological students. One result of the violence — as well as of the increasing conservatism of theological opinion worldwide — has been that Irish theological students and the younger clergy are more conservative, and less inclined for reconciliation than their more senior colleagues. It is therefore of the greatest importance to provide opportunities for Protestant and Roman Catholic ordinands to meet, and the School seeks to do this. Through its library and staff facilities the School acts as a theological resource centre for groups and individuals interested in unity, justice and peace. Based in Dublin, it also operates a programme in Northern Ireland, with centres in Belfast and Derry.

In the early 1970s the charismatic renewal movement drew together many Irish Christians, both Protestant and Catholic, into a relationship where a warm, even emotional sense of common fellowship overcame traditional theological differences. Out of this movement came the foundation in 1974 of the Rostrevor Christian Renewal Centre, under the leadership of the Anglican Rev. Cecil Kerr. The Centre has flourished, and has built cross-community bridges of friendship, undeterred by some of the questions of theological and sociological differences with which other groups, like the Irish School of Ecumenics, have felt obliged to wrestle. A later community, also strongly charismatic, but which works devotedly on issues of social deprivation, especially among ex-prisoners and their families, is Columba House in Derry, directed by Fr Neil Carlin.

The Cornerstone Community is a particularly lively and interesting group, situated on the Springfield Road in Belfast, whose members share a common concern for the nearby Shan-kill (Protestant) and Falls (Catholic) areas of the city. The co-leaders are Sister Mary Grant (Catholic) and the Rev. Bill Jackson (Presbyterian). Some members live at the Community's house, while others live in their own homes nearby. Encouragement is given to cross-community living, working and praying, and there is a special commitment to promoting local long-term employment.

In 1983 Michael Hurley, founder and first director of the Irish School of Ecumenics, went on to found the Columbanus Community of Reconciliation in Belfast. Bringing together features recalling the Catholic monastic tradition as well as that of the Reformed Community of Taizé, its members — both women and men from the Catholic, Anglican and Protestant traditions — make a commitment to a common rule and (apart from married couples, who may also join) to remaining unmarried for the period of their commitment, which is at least three years. The community, whose members undertake various types of service in the surrounding area, is dedicated to prayer and work for unity in the church, justice in society and peace on earth.

In Ireland, and especially in the North, couples involved in interchurch marriages (Catholic with Protestant) face great difficulties, and even dangers. There have been several sectarian murders in Belfast where the only reason for the attack was that one of the partners was seen to have "betrayed the cause" by marrying across the interchurch division. Many couples seek safety by leaving the country. But a substantial number decide to stay where they are, each partner remaining loyal to his or her own church, yet sharing so far as possible in the spiritual heritage of the other. Addressing similar couples in England in 1983 Pope John Paul said:

> You live in your marriages the hope and difficulties of the path to Christian unity. Express that hope in prayer together in the unity of love.

The Irish situation is more difficult than the English one, but two groups, working closely together, provide support and information — the Association of Inter-Church Families in the Republic and the Northern Ireland Mixed Marriage Association (NIMMA) in the North.

* * *

Can there be effective reconciliation of divided communities if children are not given an opportunity of coming to know and trust each other during their schooldays? This was the question which brought into existence All Children Together (ACT), a Northern Ireland organization dedicated to integrated education for children from different religious traditions. After years of vigorous campaigning they were able, in 1981, to found Lagan College, an integrated (i.e. Catholic and Protestant) post-primary co-educational school with a firm Christian basis which encourages the participation of the different churches in its religious education programme. In 1984 the school achieved government acceptance within the Northern Ireland educational system. Lagan College has on the whole been welcomed by the main Protestant churches, but on the Roman Catholic side the response has been muted, and it is significant that the diocese has never appointed a Catholic chaplain to the school.

Hesitant churches

What has been the official response of the Irish churches to nearly twenty years of "the Troubles"? Can Irish Christians point to their churches in pride and say: "There is the people of God witnessing under heavy pressure with a prophetic word from the Lord"? Or is Ireland simply an "area of darkness", where Christianity lies discredited?

Let us look first at the churches' record of cooperation with each other, especially across the Protestant/Catholic divide. The Irish Council of Churches (ICC) brings together in a representative council the mainline Protestant churches in a fellowship which goes back to 1923. It has friendly relations with similar councils of churches in other countries, especially with the British Council of Churches — of which, in fact, the Irish Protestant churches are members — and also with the World Council of Churches. Since 1975 Roman Catholic observers have attended the meetings of the ICC, and, particularly in the field of peace education, it works closely with the Irish Commission for Justice and Peace of the Irish Catholic hierarchy. No effective moves have ever been made to invite the Roman Catholic Church to become a member of the ICC, and indeed if that were to happen it is more than likely that some other members would be pressurized into leaving.

The Irish Protestant churches do not have bilateral dialogue relationships with the Roman Catholic Church, such as exist in many countries, although Roman Catholic observers attend meetings of the synod of the Church of Ireland (Anglican). However, over the years a series of multilateral organizations has arisen, in which one of the participants is the Roman Catholic Church while the other is the Irish Council of Churches, whose representatives are drawn from the different member churches.

The Four Church Leaders

The way towards this multilateral relationship was paved by a personal initiative of Cardinal Conway and the Methodist President the Rev. Eric Gallagher, at the end of 1967.[3] They suggested a joint request to the Irish people to pray for peace and work for it. The Anglican primate and the Presbyterian moderator responded positively and on 1 January 1968 the appeal was published, and attracted much attention. At that point "the Four Church Leaders" — as their group later came to be called — had not physically met together, but had worked by phone and writing. They soon did meet, however, and over the years, the regular appearances of the four leaders together with their occasional pronouncements have let it be seen that dialogue and friendly relationships are possible.

The new relationship established by the four church leaders was soon to be put to the test, for it was only a year later that large-scale violence erupted, as we have seen, during the People's Democracy march from Belfast to Derry at New Year 1969. In the following week the Anglican Primate, Presbyterian Moderator and Methodist President were invited to attend a meeting of the Irish Council of Churches (ICC) executive. They took three courageous decisions: they wrote to the Northern Ireland Prime Minister, Terence O'Neill, asking for an official inquiry to be set up into the causes of the unrest and the way it was being handled; they wrote to the press, publicly disapproving of the way the Burntollet situation had been handled by the

---

[3] For much of the information in this chapter, and throughout the book, the author is indebted to Eric Gallagher and Stanley Worrall, *Christians in Ulster 1968-1980*, Oxford University Press, 1982.

Protestant crowd and the police; and they wrote privately to Cardinal Conway, suggesting that the time had come for some form of continuing consultation regarding the political unrest and its implications for the churches.

Cardinal Conway reacted positively to this suggestion, helped in so doing by the first Irish *Directory on Ecumenism*, largely reflecting the views of Vatican II, which gave encouragement to interchurch contacts aimed at promoting peace and harmony. So in spring 1969 a semi-official ad hoc committee was set up, with nominees of the four church leaders and of the ICC. The purpose of this committee was to study the deteriorating political situation and its causes, and to advise the church leaders on whether they should issue joint statements during any particular crisis. During the terrible weeks of violence in August 1969 the committee was in almost continuous session, and made some radical suggestions, for example on the setting up of a police authority, and on the treatment of arrested suspects. The committee soon became redundant, however, when the four church leaders decided to engage in joint meetings themselves — meetings which became a regular feature of their relationship from 1969 onwards.

A highlight of their united activities was the concerted peace campaign which they launched on 12 December 1974, in which they called on their people to "let peace begin at Christmas time", and urged them to "think, pray and talk peace". In the course of a few weeks the leaders met in conference no fewer than seventeen times; the church-going public in Ireland had never before seen such clear evidence of real cooperation between the churches on a political issue, cooperation which gladly crossed the Catholic/Protestant divide.

The first official interchurch venture including both Catholics and Protestants was the Churches' Industrial Council, founded as long ago as 1956. It was mainly concerned with questions of unemployment and discrimination, and helped to secure the recognition of the Irish Congress of Trade Unions by the Stormont government.[4] In 1970 the Joint Group on Social Questions was appointed by the Irish hierarchy and the ICC, and

---

[4] Sydney D. Bailey ed., *Human Rights and Responsibilities in Britain and Ireland*, Macmillan, 1988, p.153f.

produced a number of reports, the best known being *Violence in Ireland: a Report to the Churches*, published in 1976.[5] This is a most remarkable book, representing perhaps the summit of the Irish churches' effort to arrive at a united point of view on political questions. Nothing comparable in depth and quality was produced officially in the following years, and not until the work of the Faith and Politics Group nearly ten years later were the issues raised in this report tackled in a similar transconfessional way.

Violence in Ireland asks some very radical questions: "Can the churches specify what or whose peace they seek, and spell out a concrete programme where the best efforts of well-intentioned politicians have failed? Or must they confine themselves to appeals whose vague character reflects a basic neutrality on — or even an evasion of — the concrete issues?" (p.51). And it goes on to say:

> The churches are called neither to exhortation nor to neutrality but to a positive ministry of reconciliation, costly perhaps and radical in relation to some inherited stances, and entailing active support for proposals which seem to afford a real prospect of a just, peaceful and lasting solution.

The report's recommendations are very practical ones, based on the group's unanimous conclusions. (1) "There is no justification in the present situation in Ireland for the existence of any paramilitary organizations", and similarly (2) there is no justification for the campaigns of bombing and killing. (3) The right of any group to express its views in peaceful demonstration and in seeking electoral support is upheld. (4) The churches are urged to give active support to peace and reconciliation movements. (5) They are also asked to remind their members that they have "a moral obligation to support the currently constituted authorities in Ireland against all para-military powers": this should include giving information to the authorities about para-military activities. (6) The churches are asked to support the principle of a bill of rights to protect minorities. (7) The suggestion is made that the churches should set up a Christian Centre of Social Investigation to research the problems

---

[5] Christian Journals, Belfast, and Veritas, Dublin, 1976.

underlying violence in society. (8) The churches are asked to ensure that their worship is not exploited by paramilitary organizations at funerals and commemorations.

The *Violence* report represents the high water-mark of biblical and theological thinking on political and social issues by the Irish churches working together. Unfortunately there was no effective machinery for ensuring that the recommendations were put into effect, and so the report, in the view of many critics, has done nothing beyond gathering dust for twelve years. Yet this is a harsh judgment. In fact some of the recommendations have been taken up by other groups, both unofficial and official. The Faith and Politics Group has acted as a Christian centre of social investigation, and its various documents have followed up the work of the *Violence* report. The united work of the ICC and the Irish Commission for Justice and Peace (ICJP) has produced a great deal of excellent educational material for schools on the promotion of peace and justice, as has the Irish School of Ecumenics at a more advanced academic level.

Finally, the urgent and enthusiastic commitment to working together for peace and justice which so characterizes this report has been taken up, ten years later, in the Belfast Declaration (see below p.60) around which a new movement for peace is gradually growing. The outstanding work of those who produced this far-seeing report in 1976 has not been wasted.

Ballymascanlon — the Irish Interchurch Conference

The meetings of the church leaders and the work of the Joint Group on Social Questions had by now paved the way for a wider and more permanent interchurch body. Early in 1972 the secretary of the ICC, the Rev. Norman Taggart, had contacted Cardinal Conway about the possibility of setting up a working party to discuss joint pastoral problems, including mixed marriages, and violence in Ireland. The Cardinal's reply was very positive, and in summer 1972 the hierarchy issued an invitation to the member churches of the ICC to take part in a conference at which "the whole field of ecumenism in Ireland" would be surveyed.

The Church of Ireland accepted immediately. The Presbyterian Church eventually replied that it was willing "to discuss matters of church and community relationships, especially the problem of mixed marriages and the proclamation of the gospel in Ireland, but excluding the question of church union".

The first meeting was held on 26 September 1973 at the Ballymascanlon Hotel just north of Dundalk and just south of the border — a convenient meeting place for delegates from both parts of Ireland. (It is perhaps not without significance that the carved stone coat of arms over the main hotel building — a pleasant Victorian gothic mansion — depicts a slow-stepping horse with the motto *Festina Lente*!) The media gave great publicity to the event, which eventually aroused a protest from Paisley, and led to public expectations which were much too high. It was felt that Ballymascanlon was going to be a decisive summit conference which would solve all the problems of Irish interchurch relations. As a result, a great deal of useful work which has been done by the conference's working parties has gone virtually unnoticed.

But there has been disappointment in the churches also. At various times each of the three main Protestant churches has expressed dissatisfaction with Ballymascanlon, and talked about withdrawal. The Church of Ireland especially has been concerned over the issue of mixed marriages, which represents a particular threat to its scattered members in the South and West of Ireland. In the Presbyterian Church the opposition has been based rather on the fear that somehow or other Ballymascanlon might lead to theological agreements or to shared worship which implied a denial of Reformed doctrine. Yet the Interchurch Conference has continued to exist and to provide an official multilateral interchurch forum — something which is of great importance, and which has not so far been part of the ecumenical scene in, for example, Great Britain. It is interesting that in the historic 1987 British discussions on the future of the British Council of Churches — the "interchurch process" — the Irish Interchurch Conference (Ballymascanlon) was one of the few working models proposed for their guidance. If Ballymascanlon ceased to exist, it would have to be reinvented.

Feakle

The most striking of all the church-related initiatives for peace took place in December 1974, when a number of well-known Protestant church leaders held a secret meeting with the members of the Army Council of the Provisional IRA.[6] This was after the Ulster workers' strike of May 1974, the collapse of the Sunningdale power-sharing executive, and the resumption of Direct Rule by the Westminster government. Internment without trial was still taking place, as were sectarian murders, especially of Catholics, and the Provisional IRA was being very active. Contact with the Provisionals was established by the Rev. Bill Arlow, at that time associate secretary of the Irish Council of Churches, who ascertained that the Provisional Army Council would be prepared to meet a group of Protestant clergymen from the North.

The meeting took place on 10 December 1974 at a hotel in the village of Feakle in Co. Clare (in the Republic), and among those taking part on the Protestant side were Bishop Arthur Butler of the Church of Ireland, Dr Jack Weir, clerk of assembly of the Presbyterian Church, Dr Eric Gallagher, former president of the Methodist Church, Stanley Worrall, retired headmaster of Methodist College, Belfast, and representatives of the ICC and the British Council of Churches. Those present on the Provisional side included Rory O'Brady, president of Provisional Sinn Fein, and David O'Connell and Seamus Twomey from the military wing. The churchmen appealed to the Provisionals to call off their campaign of violence, both on humanitarian grounds and because they believed the campaign could never succeed in achieving its purpose. The Provisionals expounded their aim of a federal Ireland, sought to justify their violent methods, and called for an unequivocal commitment to with- drawal from Ireland by the British government. Unfortunately the talks could not be completed, as word had got out, and they were interrupted by a visit from the Irish Gardai (police), by which time the "military" Provisionals (who were liable to arrest) had departed. The churchmen did, however, draw up a draft declaration which they hoped the British government might adopt, affirming that it had no political or territorial interests in Northern Ireland, and urging a cease-fire. This declaration was seriously considered by the Provisionals, who eventually rejected it, but did announce a cease-fire for eleven

---

[6] Gallagher and Worrall, *op. cit.*, pp.1-2,99-102.

days over Christmas. One of the Feakle group appealed directly to Andy Tyrie, the UDA leader, asking that assassinations of Catholics should cease. While he denied that such assassinations took place, there were in fact no murders of Catholics during the eleven-day period. The British army also restricted its activity. Later the IRA extended their cease-fire to 16 January 1975. It then lapsed, but on 9 February the IRA announced an indefinite cease-fire. Although this was never formally revoked on either side, it eventually broke down, the assassination of individual Catholics began again, and the IRA resumed its violent campaign.

Nevertheless this was a very significant initiative, and the brief cease-fire encouraged the British government to end the policy of internment without trial. Releases began, all internees were free by the end of 1975, and the policy of internment has never been reintroduced. The Feakle incident demanded great courage and imagination in those taking part — some of whom came under heavy criticism in their own churches afterwards for parleying with the enemy. After Feakle, the lines between the two sides became more fixed, and this promising initiative was never followed up by anything comparable.

The Pope in Ireland: "a special urgency"

In September 1979 Pope John Paul II visited Ireland. It was a memorable occasion for Catholic Ireland, where deep loyalty to the papacy is more universal than anythere else in the world, and where no such visit had ever happened before. Cardinal O Fiaich was anxious that the visit should have an ecumenical dimension, and invitations were issued to the Protestant churches for a meeting with the pope. The Presbyterian moderator had earlier made it clear that he was unwilling to attend, but the clerk of assembly, Dr Jack Weir, did meet the pope in Dublin, along with representatives of the other churches. The Protestant delegations each hoped to establish a dialogue with the pope, and previously prepared statements were eventually sent through the Papal Nuncio to the Vatican, and acknowledged. But the meeting itself was a very brief and informal one, friendly but with no opportunity for the inauguration of dialogue. Both Methodist and Presbyterian leaders had to face considerable criticism from members of their churches for meeting the pope, particularly as his Irish visit had very strong Marian overtones, marking as it did the centenary of the Marian shrine at Knock in Co. Mayo, scene of apparitions of the Virgin not unlike the modern ones at Medjugorje.

The papal visit — inspiring and renewing as it was for Irish Catholics — failed to make the ecumenical impact which might have been possible if it had been handled differently. Nevertheless some frank but friendly words of the pope to his ministerial colleagues from the other churches will long be remembered:

> Let no man ever doubt the commitment of the Catholic Church and the Apostolic See of Rome to the pursuit of the unity of Christians... I renew that commitment and that pledge today in *Ireland where reconciliation between Christians takes on a special urgency.*[7]

Chaplains to the tribe

The churches themselves are, however, part of the problem. In the words of John Morrow, leader of the Corrymeela community, the Irish churches have "become so identified with the cultural tradition, ideologies and loyalties of either Unionism or Nationalism that they are unable to help people to make a distinction between loyalty to Christ and loyalty to one's own cultural tradition". He goes on to say that they have inherited a situation in which

> the churches have acted as chaplains to two traditions which have been historically in conflict with each other. In such a role they have at best tried to restrain their followers from some of the worst excesses of their behaviour and tried to dissuade them from violence. On the other hand they have at times provided the cement by which the tradition is welded together and they have fed the deep-seated self-righteousness which prevented self-criticism and deepened the conviction that the struggle against the enemy was a "sacred cause".[8]

---

[7] *Ibid.*, p.147.

[8] John Morrow in *Northern Ireland — a Challenge to Theology*, University of Edinburgh Centre for Theology and Public Issues, Occasional Paper No. 12, 1987, pp.13,14.

As chaplains to their own community many clergy have acted with great bravery: the well-known picture comes to mind of Edward Daly, now Roman Catholic bishop of Derry, ministering to the victims of the Bloody Sunday shooting in 1972. Yet like army chaplains in war-time, they do not have much opportunity to become involved with the other side, or to work for peace. And so, in a way, the better they do their pastoral work, the more they reinforce the divisions in the community.

The Irish churches are rightly concerned with liberty and justice, and pass resolutions about South Africa or about Soviet Jewry. But when it comes to the Irish situation their concern — apart from a vague, general concern for peace — is primarily for members of their own community under pressure. Catholic priests will concentrate on wrongful arrest or detention, strip-searching, or the alleged "shoot-to-kill" policy, while Protestant clergy will protest against the inadequate security measures which allow shootings of border farmers, and bombs in towns and city streets. There have been notable exceptions to this, in particular the outspoken condemnation by the Catholic bishops of the Enniskillen bombing of November 1987, read publicly in all Catholic churches. But it is unusual to hear Protestant clergy speaking out against the incidents — which do occur — where innocent Catholics are killed or injured by the security forces. The voice of the Protestant churches has not been sufficiently raised in favour of the sharing of freedom and justice with everyone. In the words of the song "The Ould Orange Flute", Protestantism is:

the ould cause
which gave us our freedom, religion and laws.

"Papists" — in the song's terminology — are still seen as a threat to that freedom, not as equal inheritors of it.

8. A Church Wrestles with its Conscience

The Presbyterian Church and the WCC

In several ways the Presbyterian Church plays a crucial role in the Irish situation, where it represents the great non-episcopal communions which trace their history directly from the Reformation witness of both Luther and Calvin. International progress towards intercommunion or organic unity between Roman Catholics and Anglicans — for example along the lines indicated by the ARCIC reports — would still leave unresolved the great issues between the Roman Catholic Church and the non-episcopal churches of the Reformation. This distinction is instinctively recognized in Ireland where the Presbyterian Church has tended to see itself in the role of defender of the Reformed faith against all possible betrayals or modifications, whether these come from Roman Catholic claims and teaching on a variety of issues, or from Anglican teaching on the necessity of the historic episcopate — as can be seen in the slow progress of the Irish Tripartite Consultation (Anglican, Presbyterian and Methodist). Many Presbyterians therefore (as indeed many Irish Protestants of all denominations, including the Church of Ireland) see all ecumenical dialogue as leading down a slippery slope whose ultimate destination is absorption in Rome.

Presbyterians are especially vulnerable to pressure from the extreme right, notably from the Free Presbyterian Church of Ian Paisley. Neither Paisley nor his church has ever been connected with the Presbyterian Church in Ireland; yet when he started his own church in 1951, he realized that his most likely source of new members would be disgruntled Presbyterians, particularly those who were suspicious of any kind of liberalism in theology or warmth towards Roman Catholics. Presbyterian ministers in some congregations are only too aware that if they diverge too much from the accepted conservative line they may find their elders and members threatening to leave and go to the Free Presbyterians.

The Irish Presbyterian Church was a founding member of the WCC at Amsterdam in 1948. Over the years, however, ecumenical battles were fought in the general assembly, and gradually the feeling against ecumenism in general and the WCC in particular increased, the fears being both theological and political. Theologically there was the fear of "liberal modernism", and of too close a rapprochement with the Catholic (whether Anglo or Roman) and Orthodox traditions. Politically there was a somewhat vague fear of Marxism, crystallized into a distrust of anything savouring of revolutionary terrorism.

With the onset of the violence in 1969, the distrust of the WCC immediately increased, and was focused on the Special Fund of the WCC's Programme to Combat Racism (PCR), which was felt to be supporting terrorism in Rhodesia (Zimbabwe). In 1973 and 1976 the general assembly voted to continue membership of the WCC, but in 1979 a special meeting decided, by 561 votes to 393, to suspend membership, and in 1980 it was terminated.

It is worth recalling that the Irish Presbyterian Church was not alone in this: the Salvation Army in Britain also suspended its membership. It should also be noted that a very large number of ministers, elders and lay people in the Presbyterian Church continue to be fully committed to ecumenism: indeed many of the ecumenical initiatives in Ireland still come from among them. Presbyterian links with other churches continue through membership of the ICC, the British Council of Churches, the Conference of European Churches and the World Alliance of Reformed Churches. The Presbyterian Church responded to the WCC's request for an assessment of the Lima report on *Baptism Eucharist and Ministry* (1982). Yet many Presbyterians are greatly saddened by the fact that their church's action has removed them from the active fellowship of the Council. A battle for the heart and soul of the church has been joined — not primarily on the issue of WCC membership, but over the twin questions of reconciliation and of faithfulness to "the faith once delivered to the saints". Do the special circumstances in Ireland make it impossible for these two ideals to be held together in a church without dividing it?

Battle for the soul of a church

The Presbyterian tradition is a democratic one, with elected moderators of the general assembly holding office for only one year. In doctrinal matters, scripture is regarded as the supreme standard, indeed as "the only rule to direct us" in how we should "glorify God and enjoy him" (Westminster Shorter Catechism). The Westminster Confession of 1647, vitally important as it is for Irish Presbyterians, is only a "subordinate" standard. And the language of the *Standards of the Church* in its assertion of "the inalienable right of private judgment" has resonances very close to the language of the American constitution, with whose drafting several Irish Presbyterians or "Scots-Irish" were closely associated. The Christian

> is not to set his reason above the mind of God, or to refuse light from any quarter. Guided by the Holy Spirit, he is to use his reason to ascertain the Divine Will as revealed in Scripture, and he is to refuse to subject conscience to any authority but that of the Word of God.

The *Standards* go on to assert that "civil rulers... ought not to attempt in any way to constrain men's religious beliefs, or invade the rights of conscience". The words enshrine a stout spirit of independence, and of resistance to pressures — from church and state — which would hinder obedience to the message of scripture.

That is a fine tradition. And for Irish Presbyterians it raises a basic question: are they to remain faithful to their great tradition — the tradition of free speech, freedom of conscience, and obedience, under the Spirit, to the supreme authority of God speaking through scripture — or are they to allow themselves to become the tools of a tribal, communal theology which is unwilling to grant to others the rights and privileges which it claims for itself?

There are many in the Presbyterian Church who are prepared to maintain the church's historic stand for liberty against the tyranny of those who would claim freedom and rights for only one section of the community. There is, for example, the Open Door Fellowship, founded after the withdrawal from the WCC for Presbyterians who want to keep open the doors of communication with other churches. It has a fine motto: "All who are in Christ are one in Christ." And in 1982 the assembly itself passed two very positive resolutions, one welcoming "the overwhelming desire to show love and friendship to Roman Catholics by Presbyterians in Ireland", and the other encouraging "cooperation with Roman Catholics in matters of mutual interest, provided that the principles of the Reformed Faith are not in any way compromised". And following the Anglo-Irish Agreement of November 1985, a group of 24 ministers published a letter in which they made a strong statement on the indivisibility of human rights:

> It is our conviction that it is foreign to the mind of Christ for the Christians of this island to become the advocates of the rights of one community to the exclusion of the other. Those who seek peace must also seek justice for all the people of Ireland.

But there have also been setbacks. In 1986 a resolution of the Interchurch Relations Board urged the church to "engage in more positive and meaningful interchurch relationships and activities *and to give expression to this in joint worship and witness*, wherever possible, with due regard for our Church's doctrinal standards". An amendment was proposed deleting the words italicized, and this was carried by 207 votes to 146. The fear of compromising one's faith by becoming involved in any way in shared worship — using a liturgy reflecting a different theology — runs deep. On the positive side, however, this same assembly passed a resolution commending the work of the Irish School of Ecumenics to the prayers, interest and support of the whole church.

Yet another problem for Presbyterian ecumenical relations is posed by the Westminster Confession itself, whose 1647 language reflects in places the polemical theology of the time, particularly in reference to the pope as the "antichrist" and "man of sin" of 2 Thessalonians 2 (*Westminster Confession xxv.6*). What do twentieth-century Christians do about such skeletons in their cupboards? Presbyterians in the USA have deleted or amended sections of the Confession which they find objectionable. In Scotland a "Declaratory Act" gives some freedom of interpretation. In some churches, such situations are dealt with by convenient "forgetting". In Ireland, however, attempts to deal with the question have usually been met with hostility, and the warning that Reformed standards were being threatened. At times, indeed, it has looked as though the "subordinate" standard has become supreme, so that even scripture must be interpreted only in the light of the Westminster Confession. At the 1987 general assembly a first step was taken towards releasing the church from this dilemma by a proposal freeing subscribers to the Confession — all ministers and elders — from specific identification or interpretation of the offending phrases.

The debate continues...

We have dealt in some detail with the struggle in the Presbyterian Church because, perhaps more than the other churches, the decision-making process reflects the influence of the laity, the farmers, housewives, workers in factories, offices and the professions whose minds and hearts need to be convinced, who have suffered heavily in the violence, and who ultimately have to live alongside their Roman Catholic neighbours. If the churches in Ireland have some positive contribution to make in the present crisis, these are the people who must be convinced that there *is* a way forward.

9. Speaking Out Together

The internal struggle of each church, as it seeks to work out the theological and practical implications of the Irish situation, is of prime importance. But it must be accompanied by the development of structures by which the Irish churches, Catholic and Protestant, can speak a prophetic word *together* on the political situation. Above all there must be the *will* to speak and act together. The churches are very ready to make detailed statements individually, but joint statements relating to the political situation — and in practice this means statements either from the four church leaders or from the Ballymascanlon Interchurch Conference — are usually couched in very general terms, simply condemning violence and calling for united prayer and action. This is understandable, when one considers that in Northern Ireland the political aspirations of the two communities are radically different, the Roman Catholics, as nationalists, hoping for the ultimate unification of Ireland, and the Protestants, as unionists, hoping for the preservation of the link with the British crown. Added to the difficulty is the fact that the Presbyterian and Methodist church leaders (moderator and president) hold office for only one year, and that, in the Presbyterian Church, the general assembly, which meets only in June each year, is the only body which can speak officially for the church without fear of challenge.

The Inter-Church Group on Faith and Politics

At the Greenhills ecumenical conference in 1983, arising out of a paper read by Fr Brian Lennon SJ, a motion was passed calling for the setting up of a Christian Centre for Political Development, to analyze the relationship of churches to politics in Ireland, and to promote appropriate changes in this area. A steering committee was organized, and several people co-opted in an individual capacity. In the event the centre did not materialize; and as the work developed, the Greenhills conference itself, with which the leaders of the four main churches were fairly closely associated, decided that its name should not be linked with the project: official caution was evident. However, the work of the group went on, under the sponsorship of the Corrymeela Community, the Glencree Centre for Reconciliation, and the Irish School of Ecumenics, and in January 1985 it produced its first booklet, *Breaking Down the Enmity*.[1] The group includes Catholics and Protestants from North and South, clergy and laity, men and women. The drafting of documents has mainly been done by Fr Brian Lennon SJ and Dr David Stevens of the Irish Council of Churches, but each document has been laboriously hammered out by the members of the group.

Breaking Down the Enmity begins by analyzing the *fear* which is such a dominant feature of life in Ireland — the religious, political, cultural and economic fears of Northern Protestants, Northern Catholics, Southern Protestants, and Southern Catholics respectively, and also British fears. It looks courageously at the "almost tribal *enmity*" which is felt between communities. In the Old Testament God's anger is directed principally at two things: worshipping false gods and oppression of neighbours. Yet these are two features which today mark the life of those who claim to be the covenant people in Ireland: the false, tribal gods of unionism and nationalism make claims and are awarded a loyalty which should be given only to Christ, the Lord of the church. And oppression is practised: the injustice of institutional violence, and of terrorist counter-violence. The covenant community should instead be living the life of the kingdom, where "domination gives way to service" (2.4.5); the tribal idolatry of seeking the good of only one community must yield to the life of the new kingdom community, where people live for each other.

Irish Christians need to find ways of releasing themselves from the captivities of the tribal idolatry of Catholicism/ nationalism and Protestantism/unionism/Orange Order. A church's concern should be with the whole of society, not just a part of it, and each church must be helped to break free from "anxiously trying to defend an exclusive faith, rather than allowing ourselves to be caught up by Christ in his mission of reconciliation" (3.8.1). For Christians republicanism or loyalism cannot have the same claim to allegiance as following Christ (5.2).

---

[1] *Breaking down the Enmity* is reprinted in *Choose Life: Christian Responses to the Northern Ireland Conflict*, an Interchurch Group on Faith and Politics, 8 Upper Crescent, Belfast 7, 1986.

The final section outlines certain "political realities" which the authors feel must be taken into consideration in any political solution. It is interesting to note that a number of these were in fact included in the Anglo-Irish Agreement which was signed at the end of 1985, such as the recognition of the separate identities of the two communities, the continuing existence of Northern Ireland as an administrative unit, and the participation of both the London and Dublin governments in the future of Northern Ireland. There is also the significant sentence that "it would obviously be necessary to convince both communities within Northern Ireland that any proposed changes are just" (6.4.3). The Anglo-Irish negotiators unfortunately failed to persuade the unionist community of the justice of the proposed agreement, and "Ulster Says No" was the result.

The Faith and Politics Group's next task was the drafting of a Christian response to the Anglo-Irish Agreement, published in March 1986 with the title *Understanding the Signs of the Times*. This brief document (seven pages) did not commit itself to approval or disapproval of the Agreement: the question was rather whether the Agreement would help towards achieving the ideal of reconciliation and justice in Ireland. The Group's attitude towards the Agreement was, however, a positive one, asserting that "things will never be the same again in Northern Ireland whether the agreement works or not. There is no way back... The *fact* of the Agreement... confronts us with an opportunity to face reality and to change course, or else be sucked into further destructive conflict."

"Facing reality" is a key concept of the document. If the Protestant community finds the Agreement unacceptable, it must offer an alternative, acceptable to both communities (3.2). The only way of creating a future is to be prepared to lose something of oneself (3.5), by ensuring for the minority community all the rights and privileges which one justifiably claims for oneself. For Catholics, facing reality means deciding which is more important in the immediate future: a united Ireland, or justice and reconciliation in Northern Ireland (4.3). For the Republic, facing reality means accepting the fact that consent is not available for a united Ireland at this point, and is unlikely for a long time to come (7.1).

Finally, Christians must take their stand "outside the camp" of any political party and be loyal primarily to Jesus Christ who died outside his political and religious "camp" (Heb. 13:13). Followers of Christ have a *prophetic* vocation also to set each other free from the prison which they have built for themselves: "as prophets we are called to challenge each other to move out of our situation of brokenness and division" (9.3).

* * *

Ulster was still saying "No" to the Agreement. On 3 March 1986 there was a unionist-organized "day of action" in Northern Ireland, a day recalling the Ulster Workers' strike of 1974: virtually all public activity, industry and transport, was brought to a halt, roads were blocked, and a vast protest rally, addressed by the unionist leaders James Molyneaux and Ian Paisley, was held outside the city hall in Belfast. It was clear that, as part of the "Ulster Says No" campaign against the Anglo-Irish Agreement, heavy pressure was going to be put on Protestants to give public support to that campaign. The claims and pressures of sectarian loyalty were making it difficult for any other voice to be heard: the idolatry spoken of in *Breaking Down the Enmity* was becoming more and more manifest.

At this juncture a number of very senior churchmen in Northern Ireland, Bishop Cahal Daly of the Roman Catholic Church, Bishop Arthur Butler of the Church of Ireland, Dr Tom Patterson of the Presbyterian Church and Dr Eric Gallagher of the Methodist, felt themselves impelled to draw up a short *Declaration of Faith and Commitment*, pointing out to Christians of all the churches the danger of allowing political idolatries to over-ride their loyalty to Jesus Christ. The situation was comparable to that which urged the German Confessing Church in 1934 to draw up the Barmen Declaration, protesting against the claims of Hitler and the Nazi party. Reference was also made to the Kairos document in South Africa, and in fact both these documents were carefully studied in the drafting of what has come to be known as the *Belfast Declaration*. The group of senior churchmen brought the Faith and Politics Group into consultation, and the resulting declaration was published in June 1986. The document is an important and even historic one, consisting simply of four short paragraphs, followed by four pages outlining its "Scriptural Basis and Underlying Reasons". As printed, it was signed by more than fifty people, clergy and laity, from the different churches. All the signatories were from Northern Ireland, as it was felt that the document should be a Northern one, rather than one representing the whole island. The signatories pledged themselves "to God and to each other" and urgently invited others to join with them in the declaration and commitment.

The main thrust of the declaration is to protest against the "false gods" of political parties, and to assert the sole Lordship of Christ over his church. There are some memorable phrases:

— We believe that for us obedience to Christ is more important than Nationalism or Unionism.
— We seek justice for everybody in our society. Therefore we claim no rights or privileges for ourselves which we are not prepared to share with our fellow citizens of other traditions.
— We reject the lie that justice can be achieved by the use of violence.
— We reject any kind of religious or political triumphalism and arrogant assertion of one's tradition in the arranging of marches, the staging of illegal demonstrations or the provocative holding of ceremonies.
— We declare that government must respect the rights of both communities and the police must impartially serve both traditions. It is the responsibility of every Christian to obey the law of the land and support the agencies of government, including the police, in the just execution of the law's requirements, unless obedience to Christ demands otherwise.
— We declare our recognition that alienation and injustice have been experienced on the part of both communities.
— We pledge ourselves to obey God's will and Word rather than give unqualified support to any political leader or manifesto, whether Nationalist or Unionist.

It is an impressive document, and one which hits equally hard at those in both communities who put tribal loyalties before their loyalty to Christ. Forty thousand copies of the declaration were circulated, and its influence continues. On the eve of St Patrick's Day (17 March) in 1987 a large interchurch congregation assembled in St Anne's Cathedral in Belfast, and reaffirmed their commitment to reconciliation in the words of the Belfast Declaration.

* * *

The three documents which we have discussed, and which were later published in a single booklet entitled *Choose Life*, were all specially related to the Northern situation. Was it not time that a more specifically Southern approach should be formulated, looking especially at the relationship between the two parts of the island in the aftermath of the Anglo-Irish Agreement? So the Faith and Politics Group — mainly through its Southern members, but with the consultation and approval of its Northern members also — produced the booklet *Towards an Island that Works: Facing Divisions in Ireland*.[2]

This document is an effort to explain to Christians in Northern Ireland the changes that have taken place in the South since 1920, and in particular the changes in the Irish Roman Catholic Church since Vatican II. The affirmation is made that "Roman Catholics no longer seek to pressure others into the Roman Church. Rather they seek to discern with them the full implications of the Christian faith" (p.8), an affirmation which, if Northern Protestants were prepared to accept it, could do much to change interchurch relations for the better.

There follows an analysis of Southern attitudes towards the North which indicates that the fears of many Northerners are greatly exaggerated. Support for Sinn Fein in the Republic is very small: in the 1987 election only 1.9 percent voted for Sinn Fein as a first preference. Even interest in a united Ireland is very limited, with a recent survey indicating that almost half of the people in the South believe that Ireland will never be united, and less than 40 percent even desire unity if it might lead to increased taxation!

A biblical section makes two notable points. The first is that Christians should not "side with the oppressed in a way that scape-goats the oppressor": "as Christians we are not called

---

[2] *Towards an Island that Works: Facing Divisions in Ireland*, an Interchurch Group on Faith and Politics, 1987.

simply to win our freedom. We are called to enter into a new relationship with the oppressor based on forgiveness, acceptance, understanding and justice" (p.7). The second point is that the whole problem demands far more than it has yet been given in the way of *prayer*. "To pray to God, who is the Father of us all, in the name of Jesus makes a 'non sense' of our historical separation and division." We must therefore seek occasions for explicitly *shared* prayer. "Prayer is too often diminished in our attempts at separate expression and it is destroyed when that separate expression deliberately excludes fellow Christians" (p.18).

Looking at "Church Realities" the booklet deals with inter-church marriages, integrated education and intercommunion. A plea is made that integrated schools should be viewed as worthwhile experiments deserving a fair trial (p.21), and that interchurch couples should be given special consideration in their desire to be able to share communion in the same church.

The question of the legitimacy of the state is discussed briefly, in view of the fact that for decades the legitimacy of Northern Ireland was denied by the South. The authors conclude that in Northern Ireland it is permissible to work for changes in the structure of the state, but not to work for its overthrow: citizens should support the state in the just execution of the law, but should at the same time expose abuses of human rights by the state. They feel that Protestant church leaders have on the whole been slow to condemn such abuses, particularly those by the security forces.

Asking the question "how should Christians act politically in Ireland?", the authors see the first priority as the development of a political process *within* Northern Ireland involving both nationalists and unionists, even if this should involve continued British sovereignty (p.33). In order to make this possible, the Dublin government should be willing, if necessary, to reduce its formal influence under the Agreement, with a view to making a positive, power-sharing alternative more acceptable to unionists. The South, they assert, does not want to take over the North, but does want to see a fair settlement involving both communities. The South is left with an agenda of developing its own pluralism and setting its own house in order, with a view to the eventual "wooing" of the North (p.34).

A key note running through the publication, and heard in its title *Towards an Island that Works*, is employment. The Troubles have greatly increased Ireland's unemployment figures, North and South, and unemployment makes young men all the more vulnerable to approaches by paramilitary organizations. Every effort needs to be made, by Irish people and their friends in other countries, to increase employment, so that Ireland really does become — in every sense — an island that works.

10. The Bible Says...

Most Irish Christians place great emphasis on the authority of scripture. Presbyterians affirm, in the words of the Westminster Shorter Catechism, that the word of God "is the *only* rule to direct us" on how we should glorify and enjoy God. And Protestants who take the step of joining in interchurch Bible study groups with Roman Catholics often discover, to their astonishment, that their Catholic friends are even more devoted to scripture than they are and, inspired still by Vatican II, come to the Bible with a zeal and a freshness which puts to shame the rather tired Protestant assumption of knowing all there is to know about the Bible. That is one good reason why we should take some time in this book to examine the biblical basis of what we are saying about ecumenical possibilities in Ireland.

There is another reason. The distinction is often drawn in Ireland between the "institutional" ecumenism of the WCC and the Vatican Secretariat for Christian Unity on the one hand, and what is called "true" or biblical ecumenism on the other. It is alleged that the "ecumenical movement" (a term of abuse) is interested only in ecclesiastical carpentry and the "merger" of declining churches, whereas biblical ecumenism is concerned for unity of doctrine, on the basis of the scriptures as the only rule of faith and practice. It is essential that this argument should not be side-stepped, but that it should be met on its own ground, by means of unassailable biblical exegesis. It will be recalled that the authors of the Belfast Declaration (following Barmen) felt it important to back up each of their statements by a brief biblical exegesis, reminiscent of the "scripture proofs" appended to the Westminster Confession or its related Shorter Catechism. We shall examine, then, a number of biblical themes which seem to be directly relevant to the Irish situation, and which provide a prophetic word for God's people in Ireland today.

1. Reconciliation (Eph. 2:13-18)

"Reconciliation", like ecumenism, is a bad word in Northern Ireland. To belong to a reconciliation community, to speak of the need for reconciliation, is to be suspected of betraying the Reformation faith. It is taken to imply compromise, the lowering of one's doctrinal standards in order to secure peace where there is no peace. The task of rehabilitating the word is an urgent one.

The situation in Ephesians is of two groups of Christians, with a high wall of traditional division between them, recalling the wall in the Temple which separated the Gentiles, on pain of death, from the area open to Jews alone. By his death, says the writer, Christ has *broken down the enmity*, "demolishing the dividing wall" (v.14). He has "killed the enmity" (v.16) through his own death. And he has reconciled *both* groups to God, so that they have become one body.

The Greek word for "reconcile" here is *apokatallassein*, whose root-meaning is to change, to make different (*allos*). The Latin *reconciliare*, which underlies the English "reconcile", literally means "to call together again", and so to bring into speaking terms with each other. That is good. But the original Greek word goes deeper: it denotes a *change* in the people concerned. They are changed from enemies to friends. And v.16 says that *both* groups are changed, so that the two together become "one new person" (v.15), so bringing peace. For the writer of the letter, this challenge to break down the enmity between Christians took priority over everything else.

In 2 Corinthians 5:18 St Paul tells the Corinthian Christians that God has entrusted to them "the ministry of reconciliation" — the *diakonia* of changing people (*katallage*), so that they become friends, not enemies: friends of God and friends of each other. God has given this duty of reconciliation, of breaking down the enmity, to us.

2. He takes us as we are (Rom. 5:6-11)

How can we share in the worship of a different tradition, and still remain loyal to the faith as we have received it? That is a question which greatly concerns many Irish Christians, especially on the Protestant side of the divide. Am I not, says a Protestant minister, compromising my ordination vows if I attend a service in a Roman Catholic Church, particularly if mass is being celebrated?

The answer to these questions lies with Christ, whose body we are. He did not insist that people should be perfect, or should conform to any human doctrinal standard before he would accept them, though he did look for serious and total commitment (Mark 10:17-22). And of course people did become new and different *after* they met him and entered into a living relationship with him. The words of acceptance, "Neither do I condemn you", were followed by words which set a new life-style: "Go your way and sin no more" (John 8:11). Christ accepts us — and our neighbours — as we are.

In Romans 4 and 5, St Paul has been writing to his Roman friends about justification by faith, about how we are brought into a right relationship with God not through the good deeds we do, but on the basis of our commitment to God in faith. And now, in Romans 5:6-11, he goes on to speak of reconciliation (like the passage we studied in Ephesians 2); and here the verb "to reconcile" is *katallassein* (v.10) and the noun for "reconcili-ation" is *katallage* (v.11). Once again the root-meaning is *change*: previously we were enemies, but now we have been changed into God's friends (v.10) through Christ's death.

Who took the initiative here? Did Christ wait for us to become examples of orthodoxy and orthopraxis before he was ready to take the initiative on our behalf? No indeed! With three parallel phrases ("while we were...") Paul describes the kairos (v.6), the crucial moment when Christ took the first step. It was while we were still weak and helpless (v.6), while we were still sinners (v.8), while we were still enemies, (v.10) that he took action to *change* us from enemies to friends, so bringing us into a new relationship with God and each other.

If Christ died for us while we were still "enemies", are we ever justified in refusing to take the step of sharing in the fellowship of prayer and worship with others for whom he died, and who are committed to him in faith?

3. Setting each other free (Acts 10:1-48)

Protestants and Catholics in Northern Ireland are locked into a situation from which they cannot free themselves. Over the years they have tried to "go it alone", living in a system of virtual apartheid. There are, of course, notable exceptions: yet the polarization persists, and there is sometimes resistance in the churches to those who try to break it down. Christians are in a position where they seem unable to free themselves.

But they can set each other free.

In Galatians 6:2 St Paul gives a simple piece of ethical teaching: "Bear one another's burdens, and so fulfill the law of Christ." Bearing each other's burdens means taking responsibility for each other; doing for each other what each cannot do for him/herself; setting each other free.

Acts 10 tells the story of the conversion of Cornelius, the Roman centurion of Caesarea. But it is also the story of a second conversion, the conversion of Peter to the universality of the gospel. Cornelius, the good pagan, the god-fearing man who was highly thought of by the Jewish community (v.22), was ready to hear the gospel of Christ. But Peter, staying at Joppa, firmly believed that the gospel was for the Jews only. Up on the rooftop of the house belonging to the tanner Simon, God gives Peter a vision: all kinds of animals, including many which Jewish law said were unclean, were displayed before him, and he was told to kill and eat. When he hesitated, he received the message: "What God has made clean you must not call common" (v.15). Peter undergoes a real ecumenical conversion, is ready to go with Cornelius's emissaries when they come to fetch him, and through the witness of his preaching Cornelius is converted. The gift of the Holy Spirit proves incontrovertibly that the Gentiles have as much right to be members of the church as the Jews. Peter and Cornelius have, through God's action, set each other free.

The situation is like that of two handcuffed prisoners, each unable to set himself free. Then one of them discovers a hacksaw blade and thinks: "This will enable me to cut through my fetters." But he is unable to use it, for his hands are bound. And then he realizes: "We can use it on each other's fetters." They set each other free.

For Peter and Cornelius the hacksaw-blade was Peter's vision on the rooftop. Does God still provide instruments for captive people to set each other free — in Northern Ireland? There *are* "instruments" which can help towards escape. Shared worship is one, when people are able to see for themselves how the Spirit comes to those who seemed "beyond the pale".[1] Community work together is another, when people come to know each other through sharing in a useful task for the good of the whole community. The great ecumenical

---

[1] A phrase which comes from the medieval English settlement of the area around Dublin, which was protected by a wooden "pale" or paling fence. "Beyond the pale" lived the unsubdued Gaelic tribes.

agreements, like BEM and ARCIC, can also help, enabling people to see honestly and clearly how close they really are to one another in their beliefs.

Movement towards Christian unity cannot be unilateral. If we are to be free, we must set each other free.

4. Pilgrimage together (Phil. 3:1-17)

Pilgrimage has recently become a dominant ecumenical "image". Instead of the old model of concentric circles, with *my* church close to God at the centre, and the others arranged at increasing distances from the true faith (and conversion to the one true faith the only way of unifying the diversity), the new model is of a shared pilgrimage.

In Old Testament times the different tribes of Israel made an annual pilgrimage to Jerusalem for the Passover. As they drew near the city, the different lines of pilgrims converged, singing with the psalmist:

> I was glad when they said to me
> "Let us go to the house of the Lord!"...
> Jerusalem, built as a city
> Which is bound firmly together,
> To which the tribes go up,
> The tribes of the Lord. (Ps. 122)

Jesus went up as a pilgrim to Jerusalem with his disciples — later joined by the Hosanna-shouting throng — knowing that for him the pilgrimage would bring suffering and death (Mark 10:32-34). He was grimly determined (Luke 9:51-53) that they should make this journey together.

In Ireland too, pilgrimage is something highly significant, for both Catholics and Protestants. For Catholics the pilgrimages are actual, uncomfortable journeys, to places like the summit of Croagh Patrick, or the island in Lough Derg. Protestants think in less concrete terms, though nowadays many of them happily join tours to the Holy Land, and Canterbury, Edinburgh, Geneva and Epworth have their devotees. For Protestants, however, pilgrimage is thought of more often in terms of a spiritual journey. It is a concept given classical form in John Bunyan's *Pilgrim's Progress* — a familiar book in Ulster Protestant piety — and compressed into Bunyan's well-known hymn:

> Who would true valour see,
> Let him come hither.

and William William's equally familiar Welsh one:

> Guide me, O Thou great Jehovah,
> Pilgrim through this barren land.

The concept of pilgrimage is also reflected in the different stages of the evangelical "way of salvation", and in the "testimony" given at many revival meetings, which is often the account of the witness's own spiritual pilgrimage.

In Philippians 3, St Paul gives *his* spiritual pilgrimage (vv.4-11), telling how he has progressed from his strict Pharisaism to the point where he counts everything as worthless compared with "the surpassing worth of knowing Christ Jesus my Lord" (v.8). Then in v.12 he goes on to confess that his pilgrimage is not yet over. He makes no claim to be perfect; that stage will come only when he experiences life beyond death. But meantime he presses on: "Forgetting what lies behind and straining forward to what lies ahead, I press on towards the goal for the prize of the upward call of God in Christ Jesus" (vv.13,14). The pilgrim journey is also a Marathon race. The goal of the race, the end of the pilgrimage is "our commonwealth in heaven", Bunyan's "celestial city" (v.20). Paul invites those who read the letter to join him in the pilgrimage: "Brothers, join in imitating me."

The goal of the pilgrimage is an eschatological one, and Christ awaits us there, though he is also the way (John 14:6). None of the churches has yet attained that goal: as "the tribes of the Lord", who call upon his name, we are all on the way. This is something much greater than a cheerful ecumenical journey to the Holy Land, or a penitential ascent of Croagh Patrick. It is God's people, coming into one pilgrim-band, with a long road still before them.

> Pray for the peace of Jerusalem!
> May they prosper who love you! (Ps. 122:6)

All who love that heavenly Jerusalem are pilgrims together. The future is better, more united than the past. And that great pilgrimage of the whole people of God can have its reflection in an Ireland which looks away from the divisions of the past and present to the completeness of the future. In the words of the Ulster poet and mystic George Russell (known as "AE"):

> We hold the Ireland in the heart
> More than the land our eyes have seen,
> And love the place *for* which we start
> More than the tale of what has been.

11. Light from any Quarter

Ecumenically-minded Irish Christians tend to assume that they are the only people who take the problem of Catholic-Protestant relations seriously. But in fact many groups of Christians have been praying, studying and working for reconciliation and peace.

The charismatic movement

The modern charismatic movement in Ireland has had a somewhat chequered ecumenical career. Since about the beginning of the century there has been a clearly defined charismatic presence in Ireland, associated especially with the Elim Pentecostal group. In the late 1960s, however, under the influence of worldwide renewal, the charismatic movement established itself in Ireland, and grew rapidly. At first it was limited to Protestant groups, but in University College, Dublin, a mixed Protestant and Catholic fellowship arose, under the leadership of Alan Mitchell, later a Presbyterian minister, which set a pattern for joint renewal groups all over the island. Those engaged in the work of these groups — like the Rev. David Bailie of Bangor — saw them as breaking down the old barriers of enmity between Protestant and Catholic, freeing them to sing with conviction:

We are one in the Spirit
We are one in the Lord.
And we pray that our unity may one day be restored.
And they'll know we are Christians by our love.

The Irish Catholic hierarchy appointed Fr Martin Tierney to monitor what was happening, and encouragement was given to great interchurch renewal meetings held at the Royal Dublin Society. Conservative people on both sides of the divide were apprehensive about such developments, which were easier in the South than in the North. But even in the North many mixed groups met regularly, and Christians experienced their oneness in the warmth of the Spirit. "Warmth" is a good word to describe the influence of the renewal movement on church relations in Ireland. Inhibitions were overcome, barriers were broken down, and Catholics and Protestants found each other as people and as Christians.

The leaders of the churches, however, and especially of the Roman Catholic Church, began to have second thoughts. People who met for Bible study and prayer felt that they ought to have a common celebration of the eucharist. On the Protestant side not a few came from groups like the Brethren where "breaking of bread" was common, and did not require an ordained minister. In a predominantly Catholic group, if a priest *did* celebrate the eucharist the non-Catholics felt excluded. And so, gradually, the interchurch house meetings became less common, and Catholic and Protestant charismatics began to go their separate ways.

Nevertheless, the influence of the charismatic movement on Irish ecumenism has been strong and lasting. Under the leadership of Cecil Kerr the Christian Renewal Centre in Rostrevor has given encouragement and spiritual renewal to some who are involved in the more strictly theological and ecclesiological side of ecumenism. For many people the barriers between the churches have first been breached through the attendance at a charismatic house group: and later some of these have gone on to deepen their understanding of theological differences through study, for example at the Irish School of Ecumenics. The charismatic movement, with its refusal to let ecclesiological differences stand in the way of the koinonia of those who are committed to Christ and living in the power of the Spirit, has given many people a determination to find theologically acceptable ways of breaking down the barriers.

Ireland and evangelical Christianity

Some people would say that Irish Evangelicalism and Protestantism are synonymous! It is certainly true that many Irish Protestants would describe themselves as evangelicals, and would intend thereby to distinguish themselves from "liberals", "modernists" or "ecumenists". They would see their distinctive witness as being no different from that of evangelicals in other countries: the supremacy and inerrancy of the Bible as source of Christian doctrine (over against tradition or speculation); the penal substitutionary theory of Christ's atoning death; the necessity for personal conversion to Christ; the Christian's obligation to witness to the faith, in order that the world may believe and experience salvation in Christ. The direct personal relationship of the believer to Christ, manifested by a life of prayer, and ultimately not dependent on — though it may be helped by — sacraments or ministry or church organization, is of central importance.

Irish Christians are accustomed to define themselves in negative terms — by what they are *not* — and evangelicals are no exception. They would see their history as going back to the New Testament through the Reformation, and therefore as drawing a clear line of demarcation between themselves and the Roman Catholic Church. Their negative self-definition would be seen in the affirmation that they are not "sacramental"; they do not believe in any kind of justification by works; they do not accept tradition as comparable with scripture as source of authority; they do not believe that prayer can be offered indirectly to God, through the Virgin Mary or the saints; they do not believe in purgatory. This negative definition is often based on an outdated understanding of the beliefs and practices of the Roman Catholic Church. On this way of looking at things, the idea of seeking some kind of unity or communion with the Roman Catholic Church is seen as a betrayal of the faith: the only possible attitude to Catholics is one of witnessing to them. Such witness should indeed be done in a friendly and loving spirit, but it should be clearly understood that it is a one-way traffic, a conferring of light in an area of darkness.

Negative definition is applied also to "liberals". Evangelicals view with suspicion much current biblical exegesis and theology; they look for proof of personal conversion; they are critical of a view of Christian mission which would put issues of justice and peace before the verbal proclamation of the gospel. They would also be critical of radical liberal views on aspects of personal ethics such as divorce, contraception, abortion and homosexuality: and indeed in these areas their views might well be closer to those of the Roman Catholic Church.

That is a picture of the traditional conservative evangelical outlook. But today evangelicals — in Ireland as elsewhere — range over a wide theological spectrum. Some indeed, for example in Paisley's Free Presbyterian Church, stand at the conservative end of the spectrum, explicitly proclaiming their total rejection of the Roman Catholic Church, and of ecumenism.

At the other end of the evangelical spectrum are considerable numbers of clergy, university graduates and others who would see their position as theologically close to that of international figures like John Stott, the late Orlando Costas and Richard Lovelace: evangelical indeed, and also committed to a scholarly open-minded understanding of their position, and ready to enter into dialogue with all those who are committed to Christ and take the missionary obligation of their faith seriously. The report of the international Evangelical/Roman Catholic Dialogue on Mission (ERCDOM), edited by John Stott and Basil Meeking, has provided a useful instrument for promoting dialogue in Ireland between evangelicals and Roman Catholics, and in May 1987 an interchurch clergy conference on the report was organized by the Irish School of Ecumenics and the Corrymeela Community, and opened up new lines of communication. An indication of the report's importance in the Irish context is that the theologically conservative but ecumenically friendly Catholic Archbishop of Dublin, Dr Kevin McNamara, wrote a sympathetic review of it shortly before his untimely death in 1987.[1]

The WCC document *Mission and Evangelism: an Ecumenical Affirmation* is also most helpful here, for it demonstrates how ecumenism is fully biblical, and is also vitally concerned with evangelism, worship, church renewal, as well as the issues of peace and justice.

An interesting feature of current evangelical witness is that several young evangelical ministers from the North are serving in parishes in the Republic, where they see their mission as being one of witnessing to the gospel through the koinonia of the congregation, in dialogue with Roman Catholics who form the vast majority of those around them. Their aim is not to proselytize: rather it is to share the Messianic message and life-style with all who are willing to meet them; and to seek — together with Roman Catholic friends — to deepen their love for and commitment to Christ. Their work is interestingly parallelled by that of several Southern members of Catholic religious orders, especially Redemptorists and Jesuits, who are living in small communities in some of the more troubled places in the

---

[1] In SPCU *Information Service*, 1986, 1 and 2, No. 60, pp.97ff.

North, like Portadown, witnessing to their faith and to the work of reconciliation and justice.

What can evangelicals contribute to the search for peace in Ireland? A very great deal. It is foolish to think that any kind of widespread and acceptable new partnership between Catholics and Protestants could ever be achieved without their participation and encouragement. Already many of them are actively sharing in this ministry of peace. One could instance many of the 24 Presbyterian ministers who responded to the Anglo-Irish Agreement by their own statement, as well as many who signed the Belfast Declaration of June 1986; or the group behind the conference in November 1984 on "The Word of God to Northern Ireland", together with the work of the *Irish Christian Study Centre*, an evangelical research group based in Belfast.[2]

Many Ulster evangelicals, however, are not yet prepared to take the first step and enter into real theological dialogue (as distinct from confrontation) with their Roman Catholic colleagues. It is here that the concept of "Pilgrim's Progress" can help. In the past evangelicals (like Catholics) have operated on the "tug-of-war" model: "You are in darkness: I am in the light. The only hope for you is to let me pull you across from darkness to light." For pilgrims it is different. We have all come from darkness, and there are still areas of darkness in our lives as individuals and as churches. But Christ is the Light, and he beckons us — all of us — to join him. As we go forward on our pilgrim way we meet with others. There are things about them we cannot accept: but our roads are converging, and now we are pilgrims together, sharing our experiences, correcting our own and each other's failures, open to each other and to the Spirit who is leading us into the truth. There is nothing to *fear* on this road: we are not committing ourselves into the power of enemies, nor even of friends: we are committing ourselves — together — to Christ.

The role of the Irish ecumenist

Ecumenism is not popular in Ulster Protestantism, although the Irish Protestant churches, as we have seen, provided many

---

[2] Cf. Donald Kennedy, *Light from any Quarter?*, Ecumenical-Evangelical Studies in World Christian Mission, Belfast, 1982.

recognized ecumenical leaders on the wider world stage, most of them first entering the interchurch field through the work of the Student Christian Movement (SCM).

In the period after about 1920, however, as the student movement split between the SCM and the more evangelical Intervarsity Fellowship, forces opposed to the Christian unity movement — which was seen as a manifestation of liberal modernism — began to organize in Ireland as elsewhere. In 1930 there was a famous heresy trial in the Presbyterian Church, when the New Testament scholar Prof. Ernest Davey was accused of departing from the standards of the church. Davey was acquitted, and went on to become principal of the theological college and moderator of the general assembly. He also became one of the earliest targets of the anti-ecumenical campaign begun by the young Ian Paisley in the early 1950s. When the British Council of Churches met in Belfast in 1952, a public meeting in the Grosvenor Hall was picketed by Paisley and his supporters, carrying placards indicating that the BCC was leading Ulster Christians simultaneously to Rome and to Moscow — no mean achievement! These two charges — of Romanizing on the one hand, and of a political stance soft towards Eastern bloc countries but hard towards the USA and South Africa — have remained at the centre of the attack ever since.

The heart of the opposition is fear: the fear of the undermining of the Protestant position, leading ultimately to submission to Rome. For many years it has been customary for ecumenical services or meetings to be picketed or interrupted. Fr Michael Hurley speaking at the Presbyterian theological college, Cardinal Willebrands and Cardinal Suenens preaching in St Anne's Anglican Cathedral in Belfast, the co-chairmen of ARCIC II Bishops Cormac Murphy O'Connor and Mark Santer, speaking at Magee College, Derry, have all run the gauntlet of abusive and even violent demonstrations. It takes courage, persistence and ingenuity to go on organizing ecumenical events year after year in such circumstances, but ecumenists to do so, both Protestant and Roman Catholic, have never been lacking. The cost is high, especially for married Protestant clergy, whose wives and children are often the objects of persecution and threatening phone calls. One cannot blame them when, like

David Armstrong, they have felt that for the sake of their families they must leave Ireland, and seek a new life elsewhere (see below p.102). Yet most have stayed on. And the quiet, constant work carried on by such people, in the Irish Council of Churches, Corrymeela, PACE (Protestant and Catholic Encounter), All Children Together, Cornerstone, Columbanus and a host of other groups is beyond praise. So is the role of ordinary parish clergy who have persisted in holding interchurch study and prayer groups and united services, and have made no secret of their support for Christian unity, and their readiness to take the first step in crossing ancient barriers.

Roman Catholic parish clergy will admit that for them it has not been so difficult to be ecumenical, since if the bishops commend ecumenism, as they do, then no one will make life difficult for clergy who follow this directive. Yet the path of the Catholic ecumenist in Northern Ireland is no easy one either, especially for bishops who have felt it right to take a public and uncomfortable stand against Republican violence. Indeed here they have taken a courageous lead which few Protestants have felt able to follow, for there have been cases of violence against innocent or unarmed Catholics, both by Protestant para-militaries and by the security forces, when Protestant protest has not been heard. Men like Bishops Cahal Daly and Edward Daly, Fr Denis Faul, Fr Hugh Murphy and the late Fr Tony Mulvey have been brave enough to incur the wrath of their own side on numerous occasions, while bearing a burden of unpopularity with the other side all the time.

The task of Irish ecumenists is, then, a difficult one. What is their positive role in the present situation? Here are three comments:

1. The *theological* task. Protestants are still unfamiliar with what really happened at Vatican II, and so are bearing false witness about what Catholics in fact believe and practise. Protestants and Catholics alike need to know more about the convergence in theology signalized by such documents as ARCIC (ARCIC II on the doctrine of salvation is especially relevant in Ireland), BEM (which has already stimulated much useful and convergent discussion, even in some unlikely quarters), *Evangelism and Mission* (which has been welcomed by many evangelicals), *Common Witness*, and ERCDOM. There is

an essential task of ecumenical education to be carried out to help Irish Christians understand the real purpose of these documents: they are instruments (the hacksaw blades!) by which Irish Catholics and Protestants can set each other free, and so embark on the next stage of their pilgrimage together.

One pioneering example of ecumenical theological education is the theological faculty at Dublin University (Trinity College). Traditionally the Divinity School at Trinity was the training place for the ministry of the Church of Ireland (Anglican). In the late 1970s, however, a revolutionary change took place, and a new ecumenical faculty, the School of Hebrew, Biblical and Theological Studies, was set up under Prof. Sean Freyne. The Church of Ireland deserves great credit for this development, which in a real sense meant a "dying to live". The new faculty is an exciting, forward-looking place, and it is only sad that it has hitherto received scant recognition from the Roman Catholic Church, whose programme of theological education for ordinands is jealously restricted to official seminaries.

A comparable widening into ecumenical dimensions had earlier taken place in two professional associations, the Irish Biblical Association and the Irish Theological Association. Theological teachers from the main churches there came to know and appreciate each other, and it was through such contacts that some of the earliest ecumenical initiatives, like the Glenstal conference, found a ready and prepared response.

2. *Justice and peace issues*. Ulster Protestants have reacted strongly against some of the WCC's emphases on these issues, as we have seen. But what about the political issues of justice, and human rights as they affect Ireland itself? Action here is difficult, and liable to incur intense opposition. It is easy for churchmen in Ulster to make *general* statements together about violence, and to make detailed statements about particular incidents separately; but for the churches to come together officially and make detailed political statements dealing with specific injustices has so far — with the honourable exception of the *Violence* report — proved virtually impossible. That is why the work of the Faith and Politics Group and of the group which produced the Belfast Declaration is so important. They are not official: but they do have well-known and highly respected names attached, and by no means all of one particular church

tradition. The work of these groups challenges the churches to united action in the future.

3. *Shared worship*. We have seen that for some Irish Protestants the sharing of worship with Roman Catholics raises acute problems — just as, indeed, most Roman Catholics before Vatican II felt bound to avoid participation in Protestant worship, even at the funerals of intimate friends. The Orange Order warns its members that they must "scrupulously avoid countenancing (by presence or otherwise) any act or ceremony of Popish worship".[3] Yet the sharing of worship, including eucharistic worship, is an essential part of the ecumenical process, and vital for the breaking down of barriers of ignorance and misunderstanding.

The Ballymascanlon conference in 1973 formulated a joint statement on the eucharist in a document which in some ways foreshadows the BEM report of 1982. One or two sentences will indicate its thrust:

> We hold unanimously that Christ is present in grace and active in the whole Eucharistic action; that when Christians receive the Eucharistic elements worthily their souls are strengthened and refreshed by the body and blood of Christ which are truly and really partaken of by the faithful in the Lord's Supper... that the bread and wine are not simply symbols or figures; that Christ is present in a personal way that may be described as sacramental; that for a life-giving encounter with Christ present, faith is necessary and essential.[4]

Similar convergence is reached on the meaning of "sacrifice" and "memorial".

It has proved more difficult, however, to persuade the churches to follow up theological convergence by actual sharing in worship. Each year during the Week of Prayer for Christian Unity (18-25 January), united services are held in many places, usually following an order of service specially adapted by the Irish hierarchy and the ICC from the international order prepared by the WCC and the Secretariat for Christian Unity.

---

[3] Quoted in Eric Gallagher and Stanley Worrall, *Christians in Ulster 1968-1980*, Oxford University Press, 1982, p.195.

[4] Cahal B. Daly and A.S. Worrall, *Ballymascanlon: an Irish Venture in Inter-Church Dialogue*, Belfast, Christian Journals, and Dublin, Veritas, 1978, p.49.

These services are, of course, specially constructed for inter-church worship, and do not represent an actual sharing in the normal liturgical worship of the different churches. At the 1983 Glenstal Liturgical Conference Fr Michael Hurley suggested the concept of "ecumenical tithing" — the undertaking, as a matter of spiritual discipline, of regular (one in ten weeks, for example) attendance at the worship service of another tradition, and urged that for Roman Catholics this should be counted as fulfilment of the mass obligation.

The annual liturgical conferences at Glenstal Abbey have sought to familiarize participants with the worship of other traditions. For some years the custom was to have eucharistic worship on two successive mornings, once Roman Catholic and on the other occasion Anglican, Presbyterian or Methodist. All members of the conference were invited to attend, and to participate so far as the rules of their church and their own conscience allowed. The 1984 conference commissioned the production of an agreed version of the "Lima liturgy", which was used in 1986 with appropriate permission and in the strictly limited confines of a liturgical conference, for a celebration of the eucharist in which Catholics and Protestants shared at the Lord's Table.

The chaplains at Trinity College, Dublin — Anglican, Roman Catholic, Presbyterian and Methodist — have in recent years set a notable example of close cooperation in their work among students. The college chapel has become a place where Christians of all traditions feel at home (see below p.101), and the influence of the Taizé Community has been strong. In 1985 the chaplains arranged a eucharist in which the Lima liturgy was used by Protestant and Catholic clergy together, the communicants sharing in all the worship except for the actual communion, when in the pain of separation they made their way to altar and table at different ends of the chapel. The Irish School of Ecumenics in all its courses promotes a study of the eucharist and eucharistic sharing. Yet there are still comparatively few Irish Christians who are really familiar with each other's traditions of worship, and misconceptions and "false witness" abound.

Such shared worship is common in many countries. In Ireland it is not, and there is sometimes opposition, even to informal interchurch groups meeting together for Bible study or prayer. It is essential for Irish ecumenists to overcome this opposition, and this can be done only by the practical provision of places and moments where shared worship can be experienced. Once it *has* been truly experienced, ecumenical conversion takes place. If I go with my Roman Catholic friend to his eucharist, share so far as I can in his experience of participation, and allow him to tell me what the service means to him, and how he meets with his Lord who is really present there, I shall never again be able to deny that he is "in Christ". And when he accompanies me to my service — perhaps a liturgy of the Word — and knows how for me the reading and preaching of the Word become the means of my really meeting that same Lord, then we *know* that we are fellow disciples, on the same pilgrimage; we do not "refuse light from any quarter"; and nothing can drive us apart.

* * *

That is the essential work of the Irish ecumenist: to be an initiator, a catalyst, pioneering a particular line of action in order that it may later be taken up by wider groups, and eventually by the churches themselves acting officially. The motto of the Irish School of Ecumenics is *floreat ut pereat*, "May it flourish in order that (its work completed) it may perish", like a grain of wheat falling into the ground and dying, and only so yielding fruit (John 12:24). The task of the ecumenist is to provide the opportunity for hitherto separated Christians to meet and begin a real dialogue; to stimulate the creation of a series of communities or groups where people from different traditions can share in Christian koinonia; and to provide a constant background of faithful prayer for all these enterprises. Having done that, the ecumenist must be ready to "die"; to step aside, or to move on to the next situation where God's summoning voice is heard.

12. Theological Issues

A religious struggle?

Are the Irish Troubles a religious or a political phenomenon? The answer must be that they are both. The origin of the political problem lies in the question of how a community of settlers relates to the earlier inhabitants of the land settled. In places like South Africa, North America and Australia race or colour was the distinguishing factor which perpetuated the separation of the two communities. In Ireland the colour question did not apply, and the racial one only to a very minor extent. But the English and Scottish "planters" of the seventeenth century were Protestants, and the Irish were Catholics: both sides were devoted to their tradition, which they believed to have a monopoly of truth, and so there was little hope of assimilation since from the first intermarriage was regarded with the gravest disfavour.

This does not mean that the Troubles in Ireland are a religious war in the sense that people are fighting about theological questions. It is true, however, that with very few exceptions all the Irish people on one side are Protestants, and all on the other side are Catholics. And the struggle is really about *power:* who, in this small part of a small island, is to control political power? Can the two sides trust each other? If one side makes concessions, or shows signs of weakness, is there any guarantee that the other side will not seize the opportunity of gaining total power, leaving the losers powerless?

A case for liberation theology?

Can we apply a Latin American type of analysis here, dividing the population of Northern Ireland into oppressors and oppressed, and then seeking to eliminate, neutralize or convert the oppressors? The trouble is that it is by no means easy to identify and separate oppressed from oppressors. Unemployment is indeed much higher in the Catholic community than in the Protestant; but that situation is being dealt with — too slowly perhaps, yet steadily — by the Fair Employment Agency and the Equal Opportunities Commission. The Protestant community, like the Catholic one, is very largely a working class community, especially in Belfast. And the same social benefits, provided by the state, apply to all. This is not a situation where the English (of whom there are very few in Northern Ireland) or the Protestant elite are the oppressors; for indeed Northern Ireland is a very egalitarian society, there are few people who could be called elitist, and those there are would include Catholics as well as Protestants.

Once again, the religious factor emerges. Neither Marxism nor even British type Labour politics has ever secured a wide following in Northern Ireland. If Labour *had* been able to create a strong base it might indeed have united the whole working class, Catholic as well as Protestant, North and South, as was the vision of James Larkin and James Conolly in the early years of the century. But that never happened: always the voting, when the crunch came, was along unionist and nationalist lines. Protestant workers, managers and owners voted together, to preserve their jobs and their business: Catholics voted together to assert their separateness from the Protestant-dominated state.

a) The proletarianization of unionism

One of the remarkable features of the past twenty years has been the way in which the leadership of unionism — in its different manifestations — has become more working class. In the later Stormont period the unionist leaders had a background in landed families (Terence O'Neill, Chichester-Clark) or affluent industry (Faulkner), and tended to be relatively liberal in their attitude towards members of the minority, as well as towards the Republic. Ian Paisley's rise to dominance represents a tougher unionism of the people, and this indeed accounts for much of his popularity. Not a few of the older, middle-class unionist leaders have found it difficult to cope with this phenomenon, and have withdrawn from the political process.

Something of a similar development has occurred within the Protestant churches, where an ecumenical, liberal — or even Barthian! — outlook is now to be found mainly among clergy who are over 40; the younger ministers who have grown up during the Troubles are inclined to represent the conservative theological outlook of their more "proletarian" upbringing, and to resist stoutly the efforts of middle-aged or elderly theological teachers to change their attitudes.

It is therefore misleading to apply a liberation theological analysis to the situation. The working class population includes both Catholic and Protestant, and they are the ones who suffer most; they live where the action is. The challenge to the churches is to find ways of enabling members of this divided proletariat to appreciate each other, and to work together for the fulfilment of many shared hopes. It is a difficult challenge. At present, the *will* for reconciliation seems to be largely a middle-class phenomenon — both Protestant and Catholic — which is constantly frustrated by the hard facts of proletarian polarization. Will it always be so? Or can the vision of a new, transformed and united community somehow become a reality for people of every social background?

b) "Brits Out": a case-study in imperialism?

The simplistic solution of the Northern Ireland problem, advocated by Sinn Fein and the Provisional IRA, is that all will be well, and the violence will cease, once the British government gives a clear undertaking to withdraw its troops and administration from Northern Ireland, as it did from India in 1947. The ongoing campaign of IRA violence is calculated to produce such weariness and reaction in Britain that the government will decide finally to wash its hands of Northern Ireland. According to this view, the British are the oppressors, and if they depart everyone will rejoice in the new-found freedom, and communal harmony will be achieved. The slogan, seen painted on many a wall, is "Brits Out!"

This is a dangerous view. For one thing — as the New Ireland Forum and the Anglo-Irish Agreement admitted — the million or so Protestants in Northern Ireland would not cease to be British if the "mere" Brits departed. And secondly, the danger of much worse violence — civil war on a hitherto unprecedented scale, accompanied by large movements of population — would almost certainly arise in the event of a premature withdrawal of British forces. The road ahead is slower and more complicated than the "liberation" scenario projects. But the longer pilgrimage could ultimately bring peace and a new concept of pluralism and reconciliation, an Ireland that is neither divided, nor unified by coercion, but "complete".

It is true that Ireland was one of the earliest British overseas colonies, and that for centuries it was ruled in a colonialist way, using patterns of administration and policing which were comparable to — and at times the prototype of — systems used in other colonies. Today, however, the evidence shows that Britain has no wish to cling to Northern Ireland in order to preserve the vestiges of empire. Indeed, the signs point the other way — to a Britain anxious to depart from Northern Ireland as soon as that can safely be done. It is true that Northern Ireland contributed notably to the Allied victory in the 1939-45 war, especially through the naval and air bases which it provided for the protection of the North Atlantic sea route. But British and NATO defence arrangements are no longer dependent on Northern Ireland's facilities. There can be little doubt that Britain would gladly withdraw once such withdrawal was felt to be ethically and politically justified. Indeed, Article 1 of the Anglo-Irish Agreement makes such a commitment clear: the two Governments (Irish and British)

> declare that, if in the future a majority of the people of Northern Ireland clearly wish for and formally consent to the establishment of a united Ireland, they will introduce and support in the respective parliaments legislation to give effect to that wish.

The main reason for the continued division of the island of Ireland is *not* British imperialism, nor even British (or NATO) defence strategy, but simply the wish of about a million Irish people in the northeastern part of the island to be permitted to continue being Irish in their own way: and for them this includes being British as well as being Protestant.

* * *

The person who has come closest to the actual practice of liberation theology in the Irish context is Fr Desmond Wilson. In the years after Vatican II he was one of the members of the Roman Catholic clergy who took up ecumenism and established friendly relations with Protestant colleagues. Curate in a parish in West Belfast, he had an opportunity to see political developments there at very close quarters, and in the autumn of 1971 he was instrumental in arranging a meeting between Eric Gallagher of the Methodist Church and three of the Provisional IRA leaders, Sean MacStiofain, Rory O'Brady and Joe Cahill. This meeting helped to bring about a fortnight's cease-fire in June and July 1972, during which the secretary of state for Northern

Ireland, William Whitelaw, held discussions with the Provisional leaders in London.

Desmond Wilson, however, became increasingly disillusioned with the churches — his own as well as the others — and in June 1975 resigned his curacy, protesting against what he felt to be the paternalistic approach of the church to the people's problems of poverty, unemployment, bad housing and violence. He felt that the paramilitary groups had given much more recognition, protection and a sense of dignity to the people than the church had.[1] Thereafter Fr Wilson became a community worker, organizing unofficial schools for children who for various reasons had dropped out of the church school system, and in general identifying himself closely with the deprived and alienated community among whom he lived. Peace, he believed, could not be achieved without political, social and economic change: and for that reason he was a severe critic of the movement of the Peace People of 1976, who, he felt, were seeking peace *without* change, and so were likely to be no more effective than the churches.

Desmond Wilson's witness is a powerful one, with a strong appeal to disadvantaged young people, and to young clergy working with them. Yet there is a fundamental difference between the Irish situation and that in Latin America. In Ireland religious division lies close to the heart of the divisions in society, and until that enmity can be broken down there is little hope of making progress on social and economic issues, as the history of the Labour movement in Northern Ireland makes clear. Catholic and Protestant working class people in Northern Ireland still find it difficult to work together for justice, because they have yet to overcome their fear of one another. Reconciliation between Christians in Ireland has indeed a special urgency.

* * *

The Irish situation, then, has features which differentiate it from other situations with which is it sometimes compared.
— It is not a case of racial discrimination, as we have seen.

---

[1] Quoted in Eric Gallagher and Stanley Worrall, *Christians in Ulster 1968-1980*, Oxford University Press, 1982, p.105.

— It is not a simple case of the wealthy oppressor exploiting the oppressed poor, for there are wealthy and poor on both sides of the divide.
— It is not a case of an imperial power wishing at all costs to hold on to the financial and strategic advantages which it gains from a colony, for there are no such advantages, and the imperial power has indicated its readiness to withdraw should a majority of the people of the "colony" wish it.
— Finally, although the problem is a political one, it has very strong religious ramifications. The Irish churches are, therefore, burdened with the heavy responsibility of helping their members to find and accept a way of resolving the problem, or at least of living with it in such a way that justice for all may be established, and reconciliation open the way for peace.

Grassroots theology is a muddy business

But in fact there are a great many people in Northern Ireland who believe that it is God's will that they should *not* allow themselves to be deceived into seeking any such reconciliation. They sincerely and honestly believe that it is their God-given duty to maintain the Christian faith exactly as they have received it, and not to countenance any dilution of that faith. This attitude can be seen on both sides of the religious divide, though it manifests itself in different ways. And the plain fact is that in Northern Ireland this is the theology of the grassroots, of factory, farm and dole-queue: more nuanced theologies are rejected as the dangerous toys of the intelligentsia.

1. Protestant perspectives

The conservative Protestant view consciously seeks to reproduce the teaching of the sixteenth-century Reformers, though indeed it is closer to the scholastic Protestantism of the seventeenth century. It ignores as superficial the changes of Vatican II, and continues the ancient polemic. The attitude is seldom if ever: "Here are Christians, different from us in many ways, but caught up with us in witnessing together to an unbelieving world." It is rather: "Here is a perversion of the Christian faith, which is causing more harm than good. There is no way in which my attitude could be anything but hostility. I could never share in Roman Catholic worship, since by doing so I would be implying that there were no serious differences in belief. My task is to witness to the truth as I have received it and to work and pray for the conversion of my Catholic fellow-countrymen."

There is no question of the sincerity of these beliefs, and they may be accompanied by real good will and friendliness towards actual people who are regarded as victims of the system. In this view, the way of doing God's will is *not* by seeking relations of friendship with a church which is regarded as apostate, but rather by seeking the conversion to evangelical Christianity of individual Roman Catholics.

The situation then is that the more religious Protestants of this type are, the less they feel able to leave their Catholic neighbours where they are. It should, of course, be added that they will view not only Catholics but other non-evangelical Protestants as being in the same category, for when the name of Christian is denied to Roman Catholics, it is equally denied to Protestants who do not share the speaker's particular view of the meaning of salvation.

Politically, such Protestants feel seriously threatened by Irish nationalism, which they identify with Irish Roman Catholicism. They fear for their own special identity, and indeed for their own existence. In the present era of violence, they believe that all the bombs, all the murders of farmers along the border, come from the Catholic nationalist community which, in their view, wishes to displace them. As they look south across the border, they see a society which they do not like, which to them appears priest-ridden, severely limited in its freedom, and sapped by a general moral slackness. The only way to survive, they feel, is by defending their small territory against all attacks in order to ensure their political integrity, and by maintaining intact their evangelical belief, without any dilution from liberal modernism or compromising "false ecumenism". The answer to the question whether Ulster Protestants are really afraid of the Roman Catholic Church is "Yes". And, on the positive side, they believe that they have a God-given mission to witness to the Reformed faith, so that ultimately the whole of Ireland — and through Ireland, the world — may be transformed through the personal commitment of all its people to Jesus Christ in evangelical faith.

2. *Catholic perspectives*

The Protestant view which we have just described is certainly not the official view of any of the mainline churches, but rather the generally held outlook of large numbers of Protestant laity, and some clergy. A comparable Irish Catholic view of Protestants would concentrate less on the religious aspects and more on the political ones. Irish Catholics, certainly in the North, *are* afraid of Protestants *politically* The reasons for this are obvious: they have inherited memories of being dispossessed by settlers who were Protestants, and with whom they have never been able to integrate; for fifty years under the Stormont government they lived as second-class citizens in their own country, with considerable discrimination and virtually no access to power; and still today they are a comparatively disadvantaged community, with a much higher rate of unemployment, living in fear of an army and police presence which is frequently hostile, and suffering from the reluctance of the majority community to grant their identity and aspirations the kind of practical recognition they would like. They see themselves as the victims of institutional violence, and would affirm that the violence of the IRA is a response to rather than the reason for the violence of the security forces. And they know that there is indeed a religious element in this, since the vast majority of the Irishmen in the security forces (RUC and UDR) are Protestant.

On the *religious* side, there certainly was a time when the Catholic desire to convert Protestants was just as lively as the Protestants' wish to convert *them*: for generations of Protestants the word "Clonard" (the Redemptorist monastery in Belfast) was synonymous with attempts at proselytism, and one does still meet sincere Catholics whose chief expectation from ecumenism is that it may lead Protestants back to Rome. Such attitudes are, however, much less frequent than they were. Since Vatican II acknowledged the status of "separated brothers" as being in some way related to the holy Catholic church there is less urgency to change them, and more readiness to accept them for what they are.

At the same time, there is undoubtedly a conviction that Protestants do not possess the wholeness, the *pleroma* of the Catholic church. Above all there is the hope that ultimately all Christians may find their true identity in communion with the pope as "focus of unity" for the universal church. Protestants suspect here a claim — implied rather than explicit — that ultimately all the churches will be absorbed into the Roman obedience. What Protestants most fear is what Catholics — no doubt very kindly — tend to assume.

On the whole, Irish Catholics — unlike Irish Protestants — are happy to leave the theological questions to the teaching authority of the church. If ecumenism is officially recommended, then it is acceptable. But so far as the *political* fear of Protestantism is concerned, each person must make up his or her mind. And if, through deciding to become involved in the armed struggle against British rule in Ireland, a young man should find himself running against the teaching of the bishops, then — in the view of at least some church-going Catholics — this is a place where individual judgment may be set against the teaching of the church and prevail. Protestants know this, and hold the Catholic Church responsible.

A "reconciled diversity" of spiritualities?

Whatever theological agreements may be reached at higher levels, the ordinary grassroots church members in Ireland will tend to judge each other by various manifestations of religious life which for theologians may rank fairly low in the hierarchy of truths, but which are nevertheless sources of controversy and misunderstanding. Protestants react extremely negatively to Marian devotions, to prayers to the saints, to the belief in purgatory, and to the theology implied in the adoration of the reserved sacrament, to name but a few. Catholics on the other hand find Protestant worship bare and empty; they are distressed by the extent to which the felt validity of some Protestant services depends on the personality of the minister; they sense hardness and exclusiveness which implies that the effectiveness of the gospel depends more on the psychological intensity of the believer's response in faith than on the glory and goodness of the Lord.

Ecumenists in Ireland, as elsewhere, have tended to steer clear of these issues as being too controversial, too hurtful, and not of sufficient theological importance to warrant serious study. The Ecumenical Society of the Blessed Virgin Mary, based in England, has done useful work in the field of

Mariology: but its ecumenical possibilities in Ireland are very limited, since Protestants cannot help seeing it as a one-way pressure group. The Ballymascanlon conference had the courage in its early days to give the study of Mariology to a working group. But more needs to be done. In an era when "shared spirituality" is viewed as a possibility between Christians and Hindus, it is important for Christians to share their deepest experiences "in the cave of the heart". The quest is not for uniformity: it is for understanding, and for the deepening of spiritual life through a realization of the richness of Christian devotion. When there has been so much misunderstanding in the past it is important to *understand*, and in love rather than bitterness to claim what is in common and probe deeper into what is disputed. Serious ecumenical study of patterns of piety and spirituality in the different traditions, coupled with a biblical and theological critique done by Catholics and Protestants together, could help many people in Ireland to rise above traditional misunderstanding, ridicule and confrontation.

Can ecumenism become a good word in Ireland?

The word "ecumenism" has provoked hostility among many Irish Protestants, particularly, but not exclusively, as a result of the unending opposition to it expressed by Ian Paisley, who regularly in his Sunday services prays explicitly against the ecumenical movement. The influence of American fundamentalism of the "moral majority" school is strong in Ulster. As a result, even those who are sympathetic to the aims of world ecumenism are often critical of the term itself, which they find an embarrassment. Can the word be redeemed?

It should not need to be, since it has good biblical roots, as indicating the whole inhabited world (oikoumene) into which God sent God's own Son (Heb. 1:6), and the "world to come" (Heb. 2:5), the New Creation to which our pilgrimage leads us. However, the word itself is not of primary importance; what *is* essential is that the gospel message, salvation in Christ, and the Messianic life-style should be available for every human being in the whole oikoumene, and that all should share *together* in this new life, with no human-made divisions separating them. All *my* privileges, all the richness and depth of my tradition and my experience should be available to you, and all yours to me.

It is important — especially in Ireland — to recognize that the scope of ecumenical activity (whether we use the word "ecumenism" or not) has historically kept widening, and must continue to widen. Up till the early 1960s the interchurch movement was largely restricted to "liberal" Protestants and Anglicans, and — through the WCC — the Eastern Orthodox. Vatican II brought in the Roman Catholics. The 1960s brought in the charismatics, both Protestant and Catholic. Conservative evangelicals have traditionally been suspicious of ecumenism, but today they are engaged in dialogue with Roman Catholics — as in the ERC-DOM consultations — even though the more conservative end of the evangelical spectrum would reject such contacts. Traditional ecumenists need to accept all this activity, geared as it is to both renewal and mission, as a valid part of their apostolate. When ecumenism comes to be seen as something in which evangelicals too are engaged, an activity in which scripture is treated with the utmost seriousness, the opposition to it is likely to decrease.

The reconciliation of memories

"Reconciliation" is another word which, thoroughly biblical as it is, arouses a hostile reaction when applied to the relations between Catholics and Protestants, nationalists and unionists. It is, nevertheless, a basic principle which *must* be applied to the Irish situation. Many people in Ulster, both Catholic and Protestant, watching the gradual process of legislative reform grinding on, yet bringing no peace, might well invert the traditional workers' slogan and say "Damn your justice, we want charity". Charity, in its biblical sense of *caritas, agape*, Christian love, is essential to the situation. Injustice must be eliminated — of course. But beyond that, more is needed: and that involves love and reconciliation, the *katallage* in which both sides are made different, as through a new relationship they become sharers in the one, new humanity (see above pp.66-67). The miracle of the ecumenical communities we have mentioned is that such reconciliation is there seen in practice, as a possibility of everyday life.

Recently, reconciliation has been given a more extended meaning, through the development of Bishop Mark Santer's phrase, "the reconciliation of memories".[2] In Ireland, as in

---

[2] A chapter-title in Mark Santer, *Their Lord and Ours*, SPCK, 1982.

many other countries, there are two communities with separate identities, separate histories, a separate "historico-mythic consciousness"[3] each defining itself more or less as the negation of the other. The Protestant community has developed a "siege mentality" taking as its symbol the 1689 Siege of Derry with its stirring message of "No Surrender", which is repeated every time a new crisis looms, most recently with the Anglo-Irish Agreement. For Roman Catholics there is a "coercion memory", a sense of having been dominated by others throughout history, focusing today on the "Brits Out" slogan. Along with this goes the memory that the only successful way to challenge domination has been to resort to violence, as at Easter 1916. These memories imprison, and the two communities are locked into them. How are they to set each other free? The identity of each has been shaped by the other, in a series of negative definitions: and in a way each depends upon the other for its survival. The question is, in Alan Falconer's words, "How might the 'anthology of memories of the other' become 'real' to each community so that responsibility for the other is taken? How might 'memory' be an experience of liberation rather than enslavement?"[4]

The answer lies in a process of reconciliation and costly forgiveness.

> Reconciliation cannot be "cheap". Reconciliation involves the recognition of the interdependence of our histories. Reconciliation entails the appropriation of each others' history, through which each empowers the other to be free. Through the reconciliation of memories a new identity is born.[5]

This would involve the use of power in a new way, to empower the powerless rather than to dominate or manipulate. At present, however, there is little sign of the two communities being willing to empower each other for freedom. There is, therefore, an opportunity for the churches to give a lead to the

---

[3] The phrase is Dr Henry Grant's. See e.g. art. "The Complex Inner Dynamics of the Northern Troubles" in *Studies*, No. 292, winter 1984, pp.272-280.
[4] In *Northern Ireland — a Challenge to Theology*, University of Edinburgh, Centre for Theology and Public Issues, Occasional Paper, No. 12, 1987, p.32.
[5] *Ibid.*, p.33.

communities. There have, indeed, been some notable steps in the right direction, like the Presbyterian Church's detailed studies on Republicanism, Loyalism and Pluralism. Many ecumenical groups have faced the problem, as in the work of the *Two Identities* group led by the Church of Ireland's Canon Eric Elliott, and the Irish School of Ecumenics' recent study *Reconciling Memories*.[6]

The quest for the reconciliation of memories has important theological implications. In both communities in Ireland, the political pressures have encouraged theological conservatism, which in turn has reinforced political opposition to "the other side". As a result, Roman Catholics have in some ways been slow to implement the findings of Vatican II. And some Protestants, especially some Presbyterians, while regarding the Roman Catholic Church as "the unreformed church" have demonstrated that they see their own church as "reformed but unreforming" — an ecclesiology which all the great Reformers would have repudiated.

The reconciliation of memories points instead to a continuing Reformation, and a theology of pilgrimage together. Such a theology starts perhaps with the theologians: but historians must play a part in it, as the work of men like T.W. Moody and his colleagues and pupils has shown. Theo Moody came from a working-class family in Belfast, who were members of the Brethren (founded in the early nineteenth century by John Nelson Darby of the Church of Ireland). His spiritual pilgrimage led him through atheism and Presbyterianism to the Society of Friends. And it was as a Quaker that he carried through a revolution in the writing of Irish history, making it the common possession of scholars of integrity of all religious and political backgrounds.

Poets too have helped, and one would think especially of the two Ulster poets, John Hewitt and Seamus Heaney, who have so sensitively plumbed the identity of Northerners, one from the Protestant, the other from the Catholic side, and shown such a deep common heritage of language, soil and experience. But the task goes wider still, through the prophetic communities like Corrymeela, and out to the churches, where the journey is more difficult, yet still to be undertaken.

---

[6] Alan Falconer ed., *Reconciling Memories*, Dublin, Columba Press, 1988.

Memory can imprison. But the Christian faith focuses on moments where memory (*anamnesis*) restores and renews, and brings alive the redeeming activity of God in the Exodus and in the passion of Christ. In Ireland too, memories *can* bring liberation. "The reconciliation of memories involves nothing less than the appropriating of the story of the 'other', in the strength of God's taking upon himself the history of mankind."[7]

Orthodoxy or agape?

The agonizing question which faces Irish Christians — and which many of them are courageously facing, though others seek to ignore it — is this: *Which is more important: the ultimate triumph of my tradition — in its doctrine and polity — or the creation of a new koinonia in which bitter memories are reconciled, and new ways of relating to the other members of the body of Christ are realized?*

Irish Christians have inherited a tradition of martyrdom, of being willing to suffer and die for their faith. They find it more difficult to live for it.

They do of course recognize that love (*agape*) is more important than orthodoxy (they are familiar from childhood with 1 Corinthians 13!). But love is too often something which must be expressed in *my* way. In the time of the Inquisition you expressed your love for the soul of a heretic by burning his body: today similar love may be expressed in explicit or implicit proselytism. It is much more difficult to embody new patterns of koinonia, to go forward together in new ways of common witness and united service.

Most Christians share St Paul's belief that although the verbalization of our orthodoxy may be angelic, if we do not have *agape* we are simply empty gongs clanging. Yet there can come a point where if Christians feels their existence is threatened, and therefore also their power of witnessing to the truth as they see it, they will view themselves as martyrs, and will see their first duty as protest and verbal witness, rather than as love for those who threaten them. And the only way in which they can be released from their situation is for the "threatener"

---

[7] *Northern Ireland — a Challenge to Theology*, p.35.

to convince them that they are *not* threatened: that they are free to witness and act as they please.

It is a situation where both sides are locked into an unnegotiable position: we are both prisoners, and cannot free ourselves. But we can free each other — like those two handcuffed prisoners with their hacksaw blade. Protestants and Catholics in Northern Ireland need to set each other free. That could lead to the creation of a new koinonia, where those on each side are accepted as they are: not for what they have been in the past, but for what they may become together in the future.

13. Where are the Prophets?

Prophets and prophets

Have there been no prophetic voices in the Irish churches, calling the people of God together across the denominational divisions, people like Dietrich Bonhoeffer in Nazi Germany, Martin Luther King in America, or Desmond Tutu in South Africa?

There has, indeed, been one towering figure in Northern Ireland for the past thirty-five years, the figure of Ian Paisley. His followers would certainly claim that he is a true prophet, telling forth the will of God against all those who seek, directly or indirectly, to subvert the Protestant faith and to sell the Protestant people of Ulster into the tyranny of their traditional enemies in the Catholic South. The biblical parallelism is all there; so is the stentorian voice, the apt symbol and witty phrase, the origin from among the people themselves, the appeal to the past, the faithfulness to traditional values.

Yet there is a striking difference from the biblical prophets like Amos and Jeremiah. The great biblical prophets were men who went against the stream, against the beliefs and practices of the people from whom they sprang, and among whom they lived. Paisley tells the people what they want to hear. He takes all the old fears and enmities, reinforces them, and turns the community back in upon itself. There is no wider vision, no acknowledgment of God's dealings with people of other traditions, with Joseph as well as Judah. There is little sign in his utterances of any real wrestling with the Word of God to plumb the depths of God's will for peace and justice and love. For a true prophetic voice Ulster turns in vain to Ian Paisley.

Prophet, priest or king?

Religious leadership in both parts of Ireland tends to follow the priestly rather than the prophetic pattern; in other words, as we have seen, the churches act as chaplains to their own tribal communities. Even the pulpit preaching in many Protestant churches, prophetic as it may sound by its vehemence and eloquence, is largely directed to the "priestly" ends of maintaining the integrity of the community, rather than to calling attention to the great issue of God's justice in a world of injustice. The Irish churches — despite their fine record in mission and relief overseas — have become domesticated.

The three largest churches have, in addition, been happy to involve themselves — in both parts of the country — in certain "kingly" attitudes and functions, through their relationships with the two states. In the South, since 1922, Protestants have been content to maintain a very low profile, and this has suited the government which has treated them generously. The Roman Catholic Church, however, representing 96 percent of the population, has exercised a great deal of pressure on the state, and continues to do so, though today in less obvious ways than before. Catholic moral principles still influence legislation, as the recent abortion and divorce referenda made clear. In the North the Protestant influence on the state has been very considerable, though it has seldom been exercised in any but an indirect way by the churches, and has operated more through the influence of the Orange Order. In the past, Presbyterian ministers have served as government ministers, though the church has now taken action to prevent its ministers from accepting such positions, and the Rev. Martin Smyth was obliged to give up his right of participating in the work of the general assembly when he became a member of parliament. Nevertheless, outside observers have not failed to notice the political functions of Martin Smyth, and more especially of Ian Paisley, and to draw the conclusion that "the church" was seeking to exercise direct influence on government. One former minister of the Methodist Church, the Rev. Robert Bradford, who became a Westminster MP, paid for his political involvement with his life. The dictum of the Stormont era, "a Protestant Parliament for a Protestant People", has not been forgotten.

The prophetic function then does not rank high in the performance of the Irish churches, which have failed to break out of the "domestic chaplain" mould; there has been not merely a failure to create, but a failure to *want* to create a new koinonia, a community of Christ's people which crosses the ancient barriers. Good relations have indeed been established and maintained at the top, and in many places there has been fine local initiative. But across the board the apartheid has been widely maintained, and the people have in the main wanted it so.

Prophetic communities

Yet there *are* prophets: not spectacular, loud, universally known figures, but quiet, unassuming, effective people who have not sought attention for themselves, but have worked rather to encourage the emergence of the kind of prophetic, Messianic, interchurch communities which the churches themselves, with their inherited inhibitions, have been unable to create. They are loyal members of their own churches, yet often they have to endure unpopularity, insecurity and persecution. In each church there have been many people, some of them in high places, who have supported and encouraged these ventures which demonstrate that in Ireland it *is* possible to create a Christian community which includes both Catholics and Protestants.

Three Protestant leaders responded in 1964 to the invitation of the then Abbot of Glenstal, Fr Joseph Dundass OSB, and as a result the series of Glenstal Liturgical Conferences began.[1] They were Dr John Armstrong, then Dean of St Patrick's Cathedral, Dublin (and successor of Jonathan Swift, author of *Gulliver's Travels*,) Dr Alex Smyth, a former Presbyterian moderator, and the Rev. Robert Nelson of the Methodist Church. From that conference many ecumenical initiatives have emerged; and in the hospitable Benedictine monastery contacts have been made and friendships formed which have endured, and which have become part of a wider network of ecumenical koinonia.

We have seen the work of Ray Davey and John Morrow at Corrymeela, of Michael Hurley at the Irish School of Ecumenics and the Columbanus Community of Reconciliation, and of Cecil Kerr at the Christian Renewal Centre at Rostrevor. There have been other initiatives, each with its prophetic figures and prophetic communities. Canon Bill Arlow of the Church of Ireland, not discouraged by the abortive Feakle initiative, going on, together with Fr Gerard Clifford of the Roman Catholic Church, starting a notable series of lectures in ecumenical themes, held alternately in St Anne's Cathedral, Belfast, and in the Servite Priory at Benburb. Archbishop Alan Buchanan of

---

[1] Quoted in Eric Gallagher and Stanley Worrall, *Christians in Ulster 1968-1980*, Oxford University Press, 1982, pp.29ff.

Dublin quietly authorizing a revolution in the centuries-old Anglican tradition of Trinity College, Dublin, so that the large and growing numbers of Roman Catholic students there might have the opportunity of having their own eucharistic worship in the college chapel. Ruth Patterson, pioneer woman minister in the Presbyterian Church, and suffering harsh opposition for that, not afraid to demonstrate that Protestant/Catholic cooperation *can* be effective, even in a tough working-class parish just outside Belfast where nearly every breadwinner, Catholic or Protestant, is out of work because of the closure of the once so promising De Lorean car factory. Jim Mehaffey, Church of Ireland bishop of Derry, courageous enough to scandalize many Protestants by cheering the Catholic home side at a football match at Brandywell on a Sunday. Eric Gallagher of the Methodist Church, and Cahal Daly, Catholic Bishop of Down and Connor, long-time personal friends, collaborators in many an ecumenical report, moving spirits behind the Belfast Declaration, outspoken and courageous year after year and suffering for it.

The prophetic initiators have by no means all been clergy. Sadie Patterson battling in the trade union movement for better conditions for workers of every background, and bringing together in her little house in the Protestant heartland a circle of friends and colleagues right across the religious spectrum. Tony Spencer and his colleagues campaigning steadfastly in All Children Together until Lagan College was able to open its doors and offer integrated education to children from both communities in a fully Christian koinonia. David Bleakley, former Labour member of the Stormont parliament, briefly minister of community affairs, now general secretary of the Irish Council of Churches and keeping it from settling down in a middle-class ghetto by his intimate concern for industrial workers and their problems, especially unemployment. John Robb, Ballymoney surgeon, member of the Republic's senate, representative of Presbyterian radicalism. Sean MacReamoinn, Dublin Catholic broadcaster, writer and Chestertonian theologian extraordinary, urging and inspiring his church to live up to the decisions of Vatican II, and only one of a notable band of media people, South and North, press, radio and TV, who are committed to reconciliation and Christian unity, and eager to promote it. Una O'Higgins O'Malley, daughter of Kevin O'Higgins, justice minister assassinated in Dublin in 1927, closely linked with the Glencree Reconciliation Community and with the Faith and Politics Group, and a woman whose wise and original counsel is sought by many in church and state, North, South and across the water. David Stevens, scientist, administrator, lay theologian of the Irish Council of Churches, whose collaboration with his Jesuit colleague Brian Lennon has proved so fruitful in the work of the Faith and Politics Group. The time would fail to tell of them all. Prophetic voices have not been lacking, and around them prophetic communities have arisen.

The ecumenical moment

These prophetic initiatives have all depended on prophetic individuals who have been prepared to take the first step, to open up a dialogue where there was none before. For David Armstrong in Limavady it meant crossing a road — the "road too wide" separating the Presbyterian Church where he was minister from the Roman Catholic one opposite, where his friend Kevin Mullen was curate. Kevin Mullen crossed the road to wish the Presbyterian congregation a happy Christmas; David Armstrong returned the compliment, and by so doing launched himself into a bitter controversy with some members of his congregation, which in the end he felt obliged to leave, for the sake of his family.

That was an "ecumenical moment", the moment when something *new* happens. Everyone has a personal collection of such moments. For me, one occurred on the first day of my directorship of the Irish School of Ecumenics. An Irish Presbyterian by birth and upbringing (though at that moment a minister of the Uniting Church in Australia), I arrived with some trepidation at Milltown Park, traditional fortress of the Irish Jesuits. And then, to my astonishment, I discovered a door with my own name on it. I was a welcome guest, no longer a stranger, but a fellow citizen of the household of faith (Eph. 2:19). Koinonia between Protestant and Catholic was a reality, not just a dream.

Another memorable ecumenical moment came at the Presbyterian general assembly in Belfast in 1985. Roman Catholic observers attend the Church of Ireland's general synod, and the meetings of the Irish Council of Churches. But the Presbyterian

Church, although at the assembly each year representatives from other churches in Ireland and overseas are invited and welcomed, has never felt able to invite a representative from the Roman Catholic Church, and moves in that direction have been discreetly suppressed with the argument "the time is not ripe". The new moderator in 1985, Dr Robert Dickinson, was known to be very conservative. But Dr Cahal Daly, the local Catholic bishop, wrote a friendly letter of greetings and good wishes to the assembly. The moderator could have ignored it, or answered it formally without reference to the assembly. Instead, he read it out in full to the assembly, and said that he would answer it cordially, adding that he was ready for anything which would advance the cause of Christ's kingdom. There was warm applause. An initiative had been taken, and responded to. And later in the year Dickinson and Bishop Daly appeared together at a large public meeting in Fitzroy Presbyterian church — a meeting noisily picketed by Paisley's followers.

Crossing the road; crossing the border; crossing a threshold; knocking on a door; writing a letter; picking up the telephone; these are the ecumenical moments which produce a response, and the pilgrimage begins: not downhill to the city of Destruction, as some suggest, but uphill to the Celestial City.

Ecumenical spaces

Ecumenical moments are vital. So too are "ecumenical spaces", especially in Northern Ireland. It can still be quite difficult to find a Protestant conference centre in the North where an ecumenical conference can be held, especially if it is known that Roman Catholic mass will be celebrated. Well-disposed site-managers are not prepared to take the risk of trouble which might ensue, and if the matter is referred to higher authority the answer usually is "No". So the places where such meetings can be held are particularly important for the ecumenical process. Corrymeela, the Christian Renewal Centre at Rostrevor, the Servite Priory at Benburb, the Columbanus Community, St Anne's Cathedral, Clonard Monastery — these are places where people can be themselves, and relax, and not be afraid that they are being watched and reported on. There are others too; and in the South, where things are easier, there are places which have become specially significant ecumenically:

the Bellinter Centre, run by the Sisters of Our Lady of Sion, near Navan; the Ballymascanlon Hotel; the Benedictine Abbey at Glenstal near Limerick and the Greenhills Convent of the Presentation Sisters near Drogheda; the Presbyterian Association in Merrion Square in Dublin; the Church of Ireland Theological College at Braemor Park; the Irish School of Ecumenics' Bea House. Holy places indeed, and good resting stages on the Pilgrimage.

14. Can the World Church Help?

Ireland has not recently attracted the continuous attention from the media, and especially the Christian media, which has been accorded to South Africa, and to some extent Latin America. There are several reasons for this. It is much harder, in Ireland, to make simplistic distinctions between "the good" and "the bad", between oppressed and oppressor. The situation has therefore been seen in other countries as one that is difficult, but not specially urgent: simmering away all the time, but only occasionally boiling over in some terrible act of violence. In addition, at least since the beginning of the Troubles in 1968, much has been done by those in power — first the Northern Ireland government (admittedly under strong pressure) and since 1973 by the British government — to set right the injustices and grievances of the minority community in the North, with the involvement, since 1985, of the Dublin government on a consultative basis.

Why does Ulster say No?

The situation today (early 1988) is that so far as the state is concerned, considerable progress has been made in dealing with what had been an internationally perceived situation of injustice against and alienation of the minority Catholic community. To an unprecedented extent the British government is working in cooperation with the government of the Republic in order to protect the rights of that minority: in addition, this cooperation has the approval of many governments throughout the world, including especially the United States. The opposition comes from two sources. First, the IRA and Sinn Fein, whose objective is to destroy British rule by violence and eventually establish an all-Ireland socialist republic. No conceivable kind of negotiated settlement would satisfy them: their objective is total victory for themselves and the establishment of their type of state in the whole of Ireland. It is necessary to remember that their numbers are comparatively small: they are kept in action only through the support of their friends overseas, mainly in America. The majority of Irish people North and South believes that a peaceful settlement, if not along the lines of the Anglo-Irish Agreement then at least by consent among the constitutional parties, is desirable, and is within reach.

Secondly, the present government is bitterly opposed by the unionist population of Northern Ireland, and there is no doubt that this includes the great majority of Protestants, in all the churches. There are many Protestants in the Alliance Party which supports the Agreement, and there would be others who feel it should be taken seriously and used as a basis for further developments. Nevertheless the great mass of Ulster Protestants support the "Ulster Says No" movement, which demands the abolition of the Agreement before any political progress can be made. Put in simple terms, this means that the effective opposition to the Anglo-Irish Agreement — seen to the outside world to be so hopeful and so reasonable — comes from the Ulster Protestant community of nearly a million Irish people. This fact must be taken seriously.

The two chief objections of the unionists are (a) that the Agreement was reached without their being consulted, and (b) that the involvement of the Dublin government, and especially the setting up of the secretariat in Belfast, is a "derogation from sovereignty". But it needs to be recognized that there is an even deeper underlying objection which is the fear of the Roman Catholic Church: it is a fear not only of being forced into a republic whose ethos is largely controlled by that church, but also of being seduced into compromising essential Reformation principles. This theological fear also needs to be taken seriously, for it raises basic ecumenical issues.

Evangelical-ecumenical dialogue

The question at issue is the nature of evangelical Protestantism, as it is found in Northern Ireland, but also as it is found in very similar form in many parts of the world, especially the United States. Over the years since the 1920s there has been a consistent rejection of each other by conservative evangelicals on the one hand and ecumenically-minded Protestants on the other. The result can be seen in the Irish Presbyterian Church's departure from the WCC in 1979. Irish evangelicals have looked on the WCC as a dangerous amalgam of Romeward-tending theology and Marxist-inspired social analysis leading to the support (real or imagined) of paramilitary revolutionary groups. And the ecumenically-minded world church has regarded Irish evangelicals — if they have paid them any attention at all — as relics of the seventeenth century, or as an offshoot of American fundamentalism.

It is time that this mutual misunderstanding was challenged. The WCC is involved in promising dialogue with many churches which are far from the mainline of Western ecumenical theology, such as evangelical and pentecostal churches in Latin America, African Independent churches, and also — from the earliest days of the modern ecumenical movement — with the Orthodox churches, whose totally different theology and spirituality have been accepted as a stimulating contribution to the ecumenical dialogue.

Irish evangelicalism has a particularly strong claim to be taken seriously. It springs from a genuine Irish root in the 1859 revival, which in a sense provided for Irish Protestants an indigenous element previously lacking through the absence of an Irish Reformation. It has a tradition of missionary service overseas which in sheer numbers can be matched by few other traditions, perhaps only by the Moravians and the Irish Roman Catholic missionary orders. And it has a strong spirituality, marked indeed by a fairly rigid Puritan ethic, yet resulting in a Christian character which is hard-working, brave, forgiving, and at the same time cheerful and humorous. The forgiving element, which might seem unexpected, is evidenced by the very numerous cases of people whose closest relatives have been murdered, but who have insisted that there should be no retribution, and who have affirmed their lack of bitterness.

It is sometimes suggested that ecumenical progress between Protestants and Roman Catholics can be made only by those who operate according to recognized standards of critical scholarship, biblical and theological. It is true that such people do find it relatively easy to reach mutual understanding, and the great ecumenical agreements of recent years have been the products of such scholarship. It must be remembered, however, that large numbers of Christians, including church leaders, who ought to be involved in the ecumenical process, do not expound the scriptures or theologize in that way. We have seen that this is largely true of the Orthodox; it is also true of many Indian Christians — where indigenous theology may combine with Western evangelicalism — of African Independent churches, and of many Christians in the Pacific area. It may be that in such cases it will sometimes be more profitable to begin the process of dialogue with the sharing of spirituality and of concern for justice rather than with exegesis or systematic theology. But in a world where the evangelical point of view is growing, and developing its own theological outreach, classical ecumenism must seek to deepen its dialogue with this movement. Such dialogue *is* happening in Ireland, sometimes with the help of ecumenically-minded people who act as catalysts, sometimes without. The important thing is that the dialogue — and especially direct Roman Catholic-Evangelical dialogue — should develop.

Understanding the new Ireland

The world church can help the Irish church situation by ensuring that accurate, up-to-date information about Ireland is available. Ireland, and in particular the Roman Catholic Church and community, suffered grievous oppression for several centuries under British rule, and it is natural still to assume that Britain is responsible for all Ireland's troubles. The memory of the persecution of Penal days, of the Potato Famine in the mid-nineteenth century, and of the Black and Tans — the notorious British soliders-turned-policemen of the 1920s — still persists, and is still cultivated especially in countries like the United States and Australia where large numbers of Irish Catholics migrated in the nineteenth century. That memory is kept fresh by more recent events like Bloody Sunday in 1972, and the death of Bobby Sands and the other hunger-strikers of the H-Blocks in 1981; and there are many Irish folk-groups whose attractive music and persuasive ballads reinforce the message. What is frequently not understood is that these memories and these ballads do not in fact represent the situation as it is today. They are in the main directed against Britain, as is indeed natural, for Britain as the sovereign power in Northern Ireland still retains ultimate responsibility for what happens there. Nevertheless the anti-discrimination legislation passed since 1973, together with Britain's declared intention to withdraw from Northern Ireland, make it clear that Britain's desire is to remove itself from the situation.

The real struggle in Northern Ireland is now an internal one, and the weight of world opinion, and especially of Christian opinion, ought to be thrown in behind those who are seeking to resolve the struggle in a peaceful and acceptable way, rather than with those who wish to prolong it indefinitely by seeking the total defeat of one side or the other. There are few, if any, people outside Northern Ireland who are prepared to do much to help the unionist community, who have therefore developed a siege-mentality, as they prepare to resist, though with no hope of anyone coming to their rescue as the "Mountjoy" did at the siege of Derry in 1689. There are, however, many people, especially in America, who are able and willing to assist the IRA in its efforts to force the British to withdraw prematurely, an event which could only precipitate even worse violence than has been seen hitherto.

The Anglo-Irish Agreement, unsatisfactory as it is to unionists, is capable of modification. The fact that it is in force, and is supported by the British government, by the government and opposition in the Republic, and by the SDLP which is the largest and most representative organ of nationalist opinion in the North, should persuade overseas supporters of Sinn Fein and the IRA that their activities are counter-productive, and are hindering the establishment of a just and peaceful society in Northern Ireland.

Social justice

The controversy in the United States over the "MacBride Principles" (formulated originally by the late Sean MacBride, veteran Irish statesman and Nobel Prize winner) should be viewed in the light of the present situation. The principles, which are directed towards redressing the much higher rate of unemployment among Catholics than among Protestants in Northern Ireland, advocate "reverse discrimination", i.e. a policy of discriminating *against* Protestants until such time as the figures reach the appropriate levels. The expectation is for US firms to adopt the principles, and to refuse to operate in Northern Ireland except under their observance. On the surface this seems a reasonable proposition. However not only the unionists and the British government, but also the SDLP and the Irish government have rejected them. In the present situation of acute and rising unemployment in Northern Ireland — over 20 percent — the application of the principles would certainly create great hardship in the Protestant community; but it would also discourage US investors and probably lead to closure of existing firms, the ending of hopes for new ones, and a still further increase in general unemployment. The principles can therefore be seen as being likely to increase suffering in Northern Ireland rather than reduce it. The Fair Employment Agency is already entrusted with the task of ensuring fair recruitment and exposing discrimination: its work would not be helped if reverse discrimination were instituted.

America, West Germany, Japan and other industrially developed nations *can* indeed help Ireland, both North and South, by increasing their investment. Northern Ireland in particular has a highly skilled work force and a record of remarkably few industrial disputes. Anything which will increase employment will help towards establishing peace.

Is Northern Ireland a country where there is a flagrant social injustice, of a kind that cries aloud for the churches of the world to respond in the way advocated by liberation theologians in Latin America? The considered answer must be "No". There are indeed large disadvantaged communities: but these exist also in the north of England, and among ethnic groups throughout Britain, and not all of them in Ulster are Catholic. If Britain is in a situation calling for the full application of liberation theology, then Ireland is too: but from the point of view of social justice it is not peculiar. So far as social welfare benefits are concerned — and these are of course the same for Catholics and Protestants — people in Northern Ireland, who are on a par with the United Kingdom, are considerably better off than those in the South.

Public opinion in Ireland, and especially in the South, is very well aware of the situation in Latin America. Large numbers of Roman Catholic missionaries, clergy, sisters and laity, are at work in these countries and in the Philippines, many of them are deeply and sacrificially involved in "base communities", and the public is kept very well informed of their activities in the cause of social justice. When President Reagan visited Ireland in 1985, the government held a gala dinner for him in Dublin Castle. Normally such an occasion would have a very large sprinkling of Catholic bishops. Somehow or other on this unique occasion all of them found other engagements to keep them from coming. It was a major snub. And the reason? The

Irish church knew too much about American policy in Nicaragua and El Salvador to be ready to associate with the man who was felt to be responsible for those policies. Yet the Irish bishops, and the vast majority of Irish Catholic clergy, however nationalist their outlook, do not look on Northern Ireland as a place where social issues are to be dealt with by political action which is other than constitutional. In the words of the Belfast Declaration: "It is our responsibility to recognize that such injustices as are now experienced by one or other community in Northern Ireland do not warrant any attempt by either to make government unworkable."

Family ethics

One of my Irish Roman Catholic colleagues, who attended the Vancouver Assembly of the WCC in 1983, said that what struck him most forcefully about the Assembly was its failure to make more than the most superficial reference to abortion. For him this was literally the most vital question facing the churches. It was also a very divisive ecumenical question in Ireland, for in 1983 a referendum was held in the Republic on whether or not to write the already existing legal prohibition of abortion into the state's constitution. Protestants in the Republic, who were little if any more in favour of abortion-on-demand than their Catholic fellow-citizens, feared nevertheless for cases in which a mother's life might be set at risk by saving the baby, and so they voted against the proposal. The debate was a very emotive one, and did much to worsen ecumenical relations. Comparable division was caused again in 1986, when a referendum was held on a proposal to relax the prohibition of divorce, which by the 1937 constitution is outlawed in the South of Ireland. Once again the majority Catholic vote prevailed, and divorce is still illegal in the Republic, though the incidence of marriage breakdowns, and also of extra-marital liaisons is probably as great in the South as in the North, where divorce is permitted.

Contraception by artificial means was also prohibited by law in the Republic until 1978, when a gradual relaxation of the rules began. The hierarchy declared that although contraception was morally wrong, it was not necessarily the state's duty to prohibit the sale of contraceptives; and Bishop Murphy of Cork in explanation said significantly that the church did not need the state to bolster up its teaching.[1]

These three matters — abortion, divorce and contraception — have frequently been cited as barriers to any rapprochement between North and South, though indeed the most religiously conservative of the "political Protestants" in the North would, in their personally approved standards, be close to the Catholic stances reflected in the Republic's legislation.

This would seem to be an area which could benefit by international ecumenical study across the Catholic-Protestant frontier, divisive though it may be. Certainly there are great differences of opinion: but there is need for *joint* discussion which is taken outside the context of an immediate controversy. In Ireland the topic was courageously introduced at the Glenstal Liturgical Conference in 1985, with a contribution by Dr John Habgood, Archbishop of York, on the whole field of genetic engineering which is still regarded as an area where Catholics and others are bound to clash. There is, however, the possibility of establishing considerable common ground in relation to the development together of an understanding of the Christian family. At a time when there has been so much convergence in the areas of faith and order on the one hand, and of peace and justice on the other, it is time for the churches to try to establish certain fundamental principles on the nature and sanctity of human life, and on basic questions of family ethics. It is not a matter simply of scientific and theological argument. Some current misunderstandings rest on matters of vocabulary and definition: for example what a Catholic describes as annulment may to a Protestant be indistinguishable from divorce. There is room for much clarification. Such a project could ultimately be helpful towards improving ecumenical relationships in Ireland.

Interchurch marriages

Interchurch marriages are a source of continuing friction between the churches in Ireland. In the South they are identified as a constant drain on the Protestant, especially Anglican,

---

[1] Quoted in Eric Gallagher and Stanley Worrall, *Christians in Ulster 1968-1980*, Oxford University Press, 1982, p.120.

population, and in the North they can involve great hardship, and even physical danger for the couples involved.

The Irish hierarchy's 1983 *Directory on Mixed Marriages*, following the 1983 Code of Canon Law, gave considerable relief for couples embarking on interchurch marriages, through the removal from the Protestant partner of the obligation to sign any undertaking, and through the recognition that the religious upbringing of the children is the joint responsibility of both parents, whose obligations "towards God and in relation to church membership are essentially of the same nature" (8.1). Encouragement was also given to the provision of joint pastoral care, Catholic and Protestant, of the marriage. Difficulties still remain, however, and the new arrangements are still far from the full reciprocity or symmetry desired by Protestants. In the matter of allowing Protestant brides to be married in their own church, for example, the Irish bishops seem to lag behind their colleagues in other countries, granting the necessary "dispensation from form" only "if serious difficulties exist" (8.5).

It is important that interchurch couples, including those who make the challenging decision to practise "double belonging", should receive the maximum possible support, and that means especially international ecumenical support. The two Irish groups, AIF (Association of Inter-Church Families) in the South and NIMMA (Northern Ireland Mixed Marriage Association) have been much helped by their links with the corresponding body in Britain, and with the Foyers mixtes in France. It is of great help to them to be aware of what is happening in other countries, in the hope that the Irish churches, and especially the Catholic Church, may not lag behind other countries in the way they interpret the official documents. Moments which cause particular pain are the exclusion of the Protestant partner from communion, or where it is made difficult for a baptism to be carried out in such a way that it can be registered in both churches. Interchurch families are indeed ecumenical pioneers, and deserve all the encouragement the world church can give them.

Can ecumenical agreements help Ireland?

Do the great international ecumenical agreements like ARCIC and BEM have a positive role in relation to Ireland? The answer is certainly "Yes", even though ARCIC I in particular has raised considerable opposition in the Church of Ireland on account of its treatment of "universal primacy" in relation to the Bishop of Rome. As we have seen, BEM has evoked a positive if critical response even from the Irish Presbyterian Church which is no longer a member of the WCC.

To some extent the international consultations and their agreed reports can act as a brake on local dialogues: why seek for a local solution to a problem of faith and order, when a package deal may one day descend from the upper storeys of international ecumenical debate? In Ireland, for example, the Tripartite Consultation of Anglicans, Methodists and Presbyterians, while diligently aware of BEM, ARCIC and the Welsh Covenant, has not been able to recover the urgency of its earlier years when it produced its own approach to a basis of union, *Towards a United Church* (1973). And it is perhaps significant that the great church unions of South India (1947), North India (1970) and Australia (1977) were all consummated before the current series of agreements began to appear. Yet the process of digging deep to uncover the common doctrinal heritage of all the churches is one which has already proved of practical value in Ireland. BEM and ARCIC have provided the material for many interchurch seminars and conferences. The "Lima liturgy" based on BEM has so far produced two Irish adaptations, one for the Tripartite Consultation, which has frequently been used at meetings of the ICC and elsewhere, and one for the Glenstal Liturgical Conference (see above p.81). The Reformed/Catholic report on *The Presence of Christ in Church and World* and the Anglican/Reformed document *God's Reign and Our Unity* have also promoted useful discussions between and within the churches. The ERCDOM report, and *Mission and Evangelism: an Ecumenical Affirmation* are, as we have seen, specially significant for evangelical/Catholic dialogue in Ireland.

Continuing reformation

Too many Irish Protestants have allowed the Reformation to become a once-for-all, distant event, which has crystallized into a permanent, virtually infallible form. The post-Reformation formularies, like the Westminster Confession, then become the key to the interpretation of scripture, in a way not very different from but less flexible than the Roman Catholic interpretation of tradition, of which Protestants are so critical. When Irish Protestants and Catholics come to realize — in the spirit of Vatican II — that reformation is something which must go on continually in the life and renewal of the church, and that such a continuing reformation is something in which Christians of all churches can share, then their whole approach to theology and to unity is transformed, and the international agreements are seen as helpful tools in the common quest for unity according to God's will. This liberating experience of the few has still to be shared by the many.

Support for ecumenical initiatives

An axiom of ecumenical work in Ireland, as no doubt in many other places, is that churches are unwilling to pay for enterprises which they do not control. It is a comparatively simple matter for a Protestant or Catholic church in Northern Ireland to raise large sums of money for the construction of a new church hall. To persuade such parishes or congregations to contribute to an ecumenical enterprise like Corrymeela or the Irish School of Ecumenics is a much more difficult proposition. Even the Irish Council of Churches, the official council linking and serving the main Protestant churches, has considerable difficulty in finding the finance it needs to carry out its work.

The most notable example of international funding for ecumenical projects is the Inter-Church Emergency Fund for Ireland, supported by the European Catholic Episcopal Conference (CCEE) and the Council of European Churches (CEC) in association with the WCC's Inter-Church Aid, Refugee and World Service programme, and administered by a joint committee of the Irish Catholic hierarchy and the Irish Council of Churches. Over the years this fund has provided very useful, if limited, financing for many ecumenical projects. More could be done, however, at the world level. Certain criteria need to be applied, since there are numerous good works, with perhaps some ecumenical content, which are controlled by a single church, and so are not fully ecumenical. To be truly effective in the Irish situation, an ecumenical organization must operate across the Catholic/Protestant divide, and must have some kind of cordial relationship, though not necessarily an institutional connection, with the main Irish churches, either directly or through the Inter-Church Conference (Ballymascanlon) or the Irish Council of Churches. Difficult but vital pioneering work has been done by the organizations and communities which have been described earlier in this book: their effectiveness could be greatly increased and their scale enlarged if they had more support from churches outside Ireland.

It will, of course, be asked, "Why don't the Irish churches pay for these ventures themselves?" The answer is that the Irish churches are part of the problem, as they are still very hesitant about practical ecumenism; these projects need support from the worldwide church precisely in order that the Irish churches may have the challenge presented to them as effectively as possible.

No pressure, please!

It is of the essence of such assistance that it should help Irish initiatives which are already in operation, and have proved their effectiveness. Schemes which are planned to suit the ideas of donor agencies, or which force hard-working and short-staffed organizations to think up new projects when what they really need is resources to survive and to develop existing programmes, can be counter-productive. It should also be remembered that not all projects need be of the kind which make an immediate appeal to the heartstrings of potential donors. Schemes for giving schoolchildren from opposing ghetto areas a holiday overseas are undoubtedly enjoyable, and create new friendships: but they are also expensive, and evanescent. It could be more significant to support an ongoing scheme, which for year after year will bring senior schoolchildren to weekend camps *in Ireland*, in a context where newly formed relationships and experiences can be developed and assessed. Programmes for long-term and regular courses in interchurch relations, like those organized by the Christian Education Movement, the ICJP/ICC Peace Education Programme, and the Irish School of Ecumenics are in special need of support, providing as they do the groundwork for ecumenical development in the future. The structure for organizing such aid at the Irish end is already in place, through the Inter-Church Emergency Fund for Ireland.

Sharing ideas

One of the ways the church in other countries can help in the Irish situation is by examples of Messianic life-style which have worked in other places and might provide a successful pattern for Ireland. And Ireland in turn can provide working models for other places, as it has in the past, right from the time of Columbanus and the Wandering Scholars of the early middle ages.

Already there are cases of the adoption and development of such overseas examples. Corrymeela was influenced by the Iona community in Scotland and especially by the Agape community in Italy, and its highly successful Summerfest draws inspiration from the German Kirchentag. The Irish School of Ecumenics has borrowed certain features from the Bossey Ecumenical Institute, though in other ways it is very different. Irish inter-church families have, as we have seen, been helped by the example of Foyers mixtes in France. The service of keeping windows open to the world is a very important one in Ireland. Each of the Irish churches keeps in touch with the methods, successes and failures of fellow members in its own world confessional family, and there are resources in the way of scholarship programmes and ministerial exchanges which help people to deepen their understanding of their own tradition. But it is important that people who have had the courage to cross interchurch frontiers should know that for them too doors for study, sharing and exchange are open. And Ireland in turn is a good seed-bed for ecumenical experiments and pilot-projects. Some schemes which seem obvious and successful in other countries are difficult to transplant to Ireland: it has proved very difficult, for example, to produce in Northern Ireland anything closely equivalent to the Local Ecumenical Projects (LEPs) with Catholic participation which flourish in England, less than 200 miles away. But if a scheme will grow in the adverse ecumenical climate of Ireland its prospects for success in other countries are good.

Missionary, come home! We need you!

Many of the leaders of the ecumenical movement in Ireland, both Catholic and Protestant, are men and women who have had overseas experience, either as missionaries in Asia, Africa or

Latin America, or in parish or educational work in the United States or Britain. In other countries they have become familiar with interchurch work; and in addition they are usually people with a strong motivation towards the church's mission in evangelism and in social outreach for peace and justice. It is an interesting example of two-way mission: the Irishman or Irishwoman working in India, Africa, Brazil or the Philippines may be learning more than he or she is teaching, and may one day have the opportunity to return to Ireland to put this wider vision into practice. There are also examples — like Doug Baker of the USA and of Corrymeela — of people from other countries who have made Ireland their home, and have contributed notably to the cause of reconciliation, as have many young volunteers who have given a year or more of their lives to working in Corrymeela or Glencree.

Lord, teach us to pray

It is obvious and easy to add prayer to the list of ways in which the church at large can help the Irish churches. But "we do not know how to pray as we should" (Rom. 8:26), and there is special need for well-informed, sensitive and united prayer for Ireland. Such prayer is not easy in Northern Ireland. People whose friends or family members have suffered death or serious injury from the violence will pray for peace; and some of those who have suffered most have given moving examples of praying for forgiveness for those who have inflicted the violence. But prayer in churches tends to consist of detailed requests for the safety and restoration of one's own community, together with very generalized prayer for peace. It is only when people from *both* communities, including those who have suffered, come *together* to pray for peace and reconciliation that the self-centredness is put aside. Then there can be and is prayer of confession which is specific and detailed, and which expresses repentance for actions and attitudes for which those praying had some real responsibility. And it comes from both communities. Such prayer is hard, and many people cannot face it, both on political grounds ("we might be praying for different political solutions") and theological ones ("I would be compromising my faith by praying with someone whose beliefs are incompatible with mine"). Ireland is an island from which a great volume of prayer is constantly arising, sincere, believing prayer. But prayer directed towards reconciliation, and arising *together* from members of both communities, is not very common, the prayer of God's pilgrim people, who have come from their different beginnings into one journeying company.

In such prayer the wider church can share. But it must be costly, demanding prayer, or it will be a superficial exercise. It is too easy, sometimes, to make a vicarious gesture which claims to be an act of penitence, without really being so. It is not uncommon, for example, for well-meaning English people to come to Ireland, seeking contact with Irish nationalists to whom they express their penitence for the wrongs England has done to Ireland down the centuries, and hoping, perhaps, to organize some kind of symbolic act of repentance and reconciliation. Such acts can cheapen the real meaning of prayer, repentance and forgiveness, unless they involve those who *today* bear the responsibility for the Protestant community in Ulster. What individuals *can* do is to monitor reactions to Ireland in their own country, and when public opinion in a particular group or church is found to be unfairly biased towards one side or the other in Ireland, to provide accurate information about the situation itself and about the many existing initiatives for reconciliation which deserve support. Prayer for Ireland can then be linked with positive action. It may be also that familiarity with what is happening in Ireland will indicate dangers of intolerance, oppression and violence already surfacing in other countries. For the Irish situation is perhaps not so much a survival from the past as a warning for the future. Techniques of violence tried out in Belfast can soon spread to Liverpool or London. The signals in Ireland, if properly read, can avert disaster elsewhere.

15. Pilgrim's Progress?

The worldwide church, then, can be of help to the Irish churches in various ways; and perhaps Ireland in turn can help other countries to understand better some of their own problems, and to find ways of resolving them. But ultimately Ireland's difficulties must be dealt with by Irish people. In the preface to the remarkable analysis of the Anglo-Irish Agreement entitled *Common Sense* (1987), the Ulster Political Research Group of the UDA made the criticism that the Agreement could not bring peace because it was only a contract between two governments "and not an agreement between those in the cockpit of the conflict — Ulster Protestants and Ulster Catholics". These are the two communities who have to live with each other, and whose present uneasy co-existence must change into something better. The story we have been hearing tells of people in both communities who have started out on the journey towards a new Ireland, and have already joined with each other in a pilgrimage together. And, like John Bunyan's pilgrims, they have many a Hill of Difficulty and Slough of Despond to meet on the way, obstacles which they cannot cross in their separation, but can face together, as they set each other free.

a) The obstacle of Catholic political fears must be overcome: the fear of the institutional violence of the security forces, the fear of their own identity not being fully recognized, the fear of being relegated to second-class citizenship, the fear of being permanently denied access to power. Various government initiatives have already provided the legislative framework for dealing with these points. But mere justice (when it is attained) will not create a new community: to it must be added the *will* of the Protestant community to accept their Catholic fellow citizens, and to ensure that they are welcome as equal partners. The fear of injustice can be banished only by the actuality of justice: and for a genuine new koinonia to emerge there must be acceptance and reconciliation. Protestants need to affirm, officially through their churches, and personally as individual Christians, that they are as ready to fight for their Catholic neighbour's rights as they are for their own. Without such an affirmation, and its realization in practice, there is no justice.

b) Protestant fears of the physical violence of the IRA and INLA must be removed. In the words of the Belfast Declaration:

> We believe that all human life is sacred. All Christians must recognize that murder is evil by whomsoever and for whatsoever reason it is committed. The sin of murder is shared by those who cooperate in it whether before, during or after its execution... We reject the lie that justice can be achieved by the use of violence.

The Protestant and Roman Catholic people of Northern Ireland must demonstrate that they have the will to resolve their differences with peace and justice, that they totally reject violence, and that they expect supporters of violence in countries outside Ireland to leave them in peace.

c) The *religious* fears of Protestants must also be allayed. This is not something which *Irish* Catholics can do on their own: there needs to be a demonstration at the highest level that the old "absorption" model has been abandoned, and that the description of the church as the pilgrim people of God really does imply that other pilgrims can join in on equal terms. There needs also to be an affirmation that the ultimate pattern of the koinonia of God's people on earth is not to be identified with any existing model, "for here we have no lasting city, but we seek the city which is to come" (Heb. 13:14). The ecumenical dialogue about the future form of the church can take place only if the question is left open: Christ is and will be the Lord and King of the church, and his followers will be guided into the appropriate pattern for ministry at local, national and universal levels. We may advocate our preferred models; but we dare not assume that one of them will displace all others. For pilgrims together the future options are still open: it is the Lord of the church to whom and with whom they are travelling, who will provide the pattern for journey's end. Meantime, however, Irish Catholics, particularly in the Republic, *can* help to banish Protestant fears by the assurance that they accept them as they are, with no pressure upon them to give up any of their civil liberties, and by according them full freedom not only to practise their faith but also to share it with others.

d) Protestants and Catholics both need to be set free to deal effectively with nominal Christianity, whether the nominal Christians are inactive Catholics or lapsed Protestants. The

Common Witness, Mission and Evangelism and *ERCDOM* documents all point towards a situation where Christians of different churches can set each other free to witness openly, wherever they live, without giving rise to the fear of proselytism. Witness to the gospel, to salvation, to social and political justice is something in which we can help each other, accepting responsibility for each other's welfare, and building a common core of committed Christians — committed first of all to Christ, and then to our own churches, yet already sharing, so far as we can, in the koinonia of the Spirit.

* * *

The churches in Ireland are still far from surmounting these obstacles; but already the prophetic communities are at work, pilot projects of future relationships between the churches as they journey towards reconciliation and full communion. If people do not wish to follow these particular models of koinonia, then other models may well come into being, particularly on the evangelical side of the ecumenical spectrum. But dialogue between fellow pilgrims there must be.

Marturia

The church is a sign of the coming kingdom, visible to all the world, and witnessing to the covenant koinonia which all Christians can share with one another. Such witness can be very uncomfortable, and many people in Ireland, Catholic and Protestant, have suffered for it. Ireland has too many political martyrs: it has sometimes seemed easier to die for Ireland than to face the long, hard task of living. The Christian koinonia today has many witnesses, "martyrs" in the literal Greek sense of those who give witness (*marturia*) to their faith. Other martyrs are pointed out as objects of veneration — the H-block victims, for example, on the nationalist side, and for loyalists Robert Bradford and others; and Paisley's vast church on the Ravenhill Road, Belfast, is called "the Martyrs' Memorial" after Protestant victims of the Reformation period. It is today essential that the witness of Christians dedicated to reconciliation and unity should be seen and heard. And that is happening: seldom in any spectacular fashion, but in the daily *marturia* of loving, serving and suffering.

Christianity discredited?

"What country do you come from?" is a question I was often asked during the years when I lived in India. And when I replied "Ireland", the next question sometimes was: "What right have you to come to India and talk to us about your Christianity when in Ireland Christians are fighting each other about religion? Hindus believe in peaceful co-existence. Why don't you go back to your own country first, and convert your fellow-countrymen?" I discovered that there was no satisfactory answer.

Christianity discredited? This book has been an attempt to face that question. Has Ireland proved conclusively that the Christian faith does not work; that the more committed people are to the church, and the higher the percentage of church-goers, the greater is the likelihood of division, hatred and violence? On the surface it looks as though the answer must be yes; and the many people who believe that secularization, as in France, or wide-ranging pluralism, as in the United States, are the only hopes for the future, can make out a strong case.

The Irish churches, on the whole, have little reason to claim that they have successfully carried out the ministry of reconciliation committed to them by God (2 Cor. 5:19). True, they have fulfilled their pastoral function admirably; and in a situation of great suffering, that is no mean achievement. They have responded generously to the cry of the hungry and diseased in the underdeveloped world. They have even, if at times somewhat tentatively, held out the hand of friendship across the Catholic/Protestant gulf, and have established a useful national Interchurch Conference. Sometimes, though rarely, they have been prepared to admit that they share some responsibility for the present situation.

But they have not been ready to make any very radical changes in their structures, their teaching standards or even the interpretation of their regulations, at least as these affect their inter-relationships. Protestants have waited in vain for a real breakthrough in the mixed marriage situation. True, there have been helpful changes; but full symmetry in relationships between the marriage partners and between the two churches has not been attained, and the Protestant partner inevitably feels disadvantaged. The hurt rankles, especially since it is common knowledge that in other European countries the rules are given a more flexible interpretation. Yet on the other side of the fence things are no better. The Presbyterian Church still allows itself to be bound to those sections of the 1647 Westminster Confession which describe the pope as antichrist. It would be too risky to change, too risky even to forget.

The churches are afraid to take risks. Especially they are afraid to take the risk of appearing to their own members to be crossing the Protestant unionist/Catholic nationalist divide; of doing anything which might indicate that they were weakening in their stern anti-Romanism or equally stern anti-Britishism. And so they play for safety: relations are correct, even friendly at the summit: but fraternizing at lower levels is a risk, and it is easier to play safe.

A new koinonia

The thesis of this book is that Irish Christians are being called by God to a new fellowship, a new koinonia, a pilgrimage together which will unite Catholic and Protestant in a single witnessing, serving community. It is not a pilgrimage which attempts to take shortcuts, to experience prematurely the fullness of communion which the churches are not yet ready to enter. But it *is* a breaking down of the enmity, a choosing of life, a step towards an island that works.

And this koinonia already exists.

We have looked at some of its manifestations, in interchurch groups of people who are committed to their churches, but also committed to each other, and to the quest for justice, for peace, for communion. Their numbers are not great, and many Irish Christians know little about them. But they represent something *new* in the history of Ireland. For the first time since the Reformation, considerable numbers of Irish Christians from both traditions have come together in a series of interlinked groups committed to their faith and to their own traditions, yet looking to a common future, and already enjoying a foretaste of what life in a "complete" Ireland might be like.

Their koinonia is committed to common witness to the faith, not merely in their pursuit of justice and peace — though that is part of the witness — but in the proclamation of the good news of Jesus the Christ, and the sharing of the Messianic life-style with all those, outside or within the churches, who do not know it. They are not interested in proselytism, which they reject; but they are vitally concerned that more and more people should experience the fullness of a Christian life anchored in personal commitment to the Lord of the church. Committed to the proclamation of the liberating word, they share in the prophetic ministry of Christ.

They are committed to the unity of Christians, and long for the day when that unity will be expressed by common participation in the bread and wine of the eucharist. But meantime, while firmly grounded in their own traditions, they share in each other's worship and prayer to the maximum possible extent. There are features of one another's traditions which they cannot accept. But they know that when they hear the Word read and preached, and when they attend each other's eucharists, it is the same Lord who is truly present to each of them. And so, already, they share in the same pilgrim life-style, looking to the future with hope because the present has enabled them to set each other free. Committed to the liturgical and corporate life of the church, they share in the priestly ministry of Christ.

They are also committed to the quest for justice and peace — in every country, but especially in Ireland. Because they are working together, not in isolation, this means that they can never approach questions of justice or peace asking simply: "How can I protect the interests of *my community*?" Justice is indivisible, and therefore they are committed to ensuring that all citizens enjoy the same rights and privileges in practice as well as on paper. This is often a painful process, involving loss of power as well as sharing of power. They seek to approach it in the way of their Master, whose kingly service meant washing his disciples' feet and going the way of the cross. Committed to the church's ministry of diakonia they share the kingly ministry of the servant Christ.

Pilgrimage together

It is not easy for a Christian group or a Christian church to serve with Christ in his threefold ministry of prophet, priest and servant-king. It is particularly difficult when this involves — as it must — service *outside* the tribe, service which goes, with Christ, "outside the camp" (Heb. 13:13). Hard-line political Protestants and Catholics, who can envisage only a one-way solution to Ireland's troubles, as well as ordinary loyal church members who are friendly to those outside their tradition, but not courageous enough to take risks, will all indicate their opposition, at best by ignoring the pilgrims, at worst by real and painful persecution. But the pilgrims know that they must keep moving forward on their journey, across all the sloughs of despond and hills of difficulty, avoiding none of them, yet never allowing discouragement to make them desert their fellow pilgrims.

The pilgrimage must be authentic — not a human creation, or somebody's bright idea, but obedience to the will of God. It is empowered by God's Spirit, and shows the fruit of the Spirit in the seriousness of its grappling with the Bible, the quality of its prayer, the joy and integrity of its Messianic life-style, the effectiveness of its witness for justice and peace, and the power of its proclamation of the gospel to those have never really accepted it. There will be converts to the ecumenical pilgrimage. And there may be martyrs.

In Ireland today, pilgrimage together is the *only* hope for Christians and churches, the only road which leads out of the sad present to the future where Christ awaits his pilgrim people. Every other activity rings hollow, and amounts only to the self-preservation or extension of the tribe, whichever tribe that happens to be. Jesus said: "If anyone wants to follow me, let him deny himself, and take up his cross, and follow me. For whoever wants to preserve his life will lose it; but whoever is ready to lose his life for my sake will find it" (Matt. 16:24-25). That implies taking a great risk, the risk of loss of identity, loss of life. But the promise is there, the promise of resurrection though death. People from the different Irish churches who have set out on this difficult pilgrimage know that nothing else they do can be equally significant for the mission of the church.

Jesus says Yes

Irish church life has long been characterized by its love of negation. Morality — Catholic and Protestant — has been a catalogue of things not to be done. Theology has had as its background Pope Pius IX's *Syllabus of Errors* and a whole series of Protestant booklets on the errors of Romanism. Censorship, constitutional prohibitions, Sabbath restrictions have set the atmosphere. "Error has no rights", "No surrender", "Not an inch", "Ulster says No": these have been the slogans, as people have sought to define their identity by indicating their difference from their rivals.

The time has come for Irish Christians of all churches to say Yes. There must of course be a No: No to violence; No to the domination of one community by another. But Yes to Christ, Yes to each other, Yes to pilgrimage. "Negative approaches have but a limited validity. It is right always to say No to what is wrong but at the same time this lays upon us the responsibility of finding and articulating a positive, right alternative. This is in tune with the Christian message of God's No to evil but his ultimate Yes and Amen to humankind in Jesus Christ."[1]

> The Son of God, Jesus Christ... was not Yes and No;
> but in him it is always Yes.
> For all the promises of God find their Yes in him (2 Cor. 1:19-20).

— Jesus calls his people to evangelism, to service, to the establishment of justice, peace and love.
— Jesus calls his people to the future, not the past.
— Jesus calls his people to pilgrimage — together.
— It's a risk.
— But in him the answer is Yes.

---

[1] John Thompson, *Religion, Morality and Politics: a Contemporary Analysis of the Northern Ireland Problem*, Presbyterian Church in Ireland, 1986.

Abbreviations

ACT	All Children Together
ARCIC	Anglican Roman Catholic International Consultation
BEM	Baptism, Eucharist and Ministry
CCEE	European Catholic Episcopal Conference
CEC	Conference of European Churches
CICARWS	Commission on Inter-Church Aid, Refugee and World Service
DUP	Democratic Unionist Party
ERCDOM	Evangelical Roman Catholic Dialogue on Mission
ICC	Irish Council of Churches
ICJP	Irish Commission for Justice and Peace
INLA	Irish National Liberation Army
IRA	Irish Republican Army
IRB	Irish Republican Brotherhood
LEP	Local Ecumenical Project
PCR	Programme to Combat Racism
Provos	Provisional IRA
RUC	Royal Ulster Constabulary
SDLP	Social Democratic and Labour Party
UDA	Ulster Defence Association
UDR	Ulster Defence Regiment
UFF	Ulster Freedom Fighters
UVF	Ulster Volunteer Force
WCC	World Council of Churches